Praise for Other Titles by Steven Furtick

"Not only does Pastor Steven give voice to the hurt we so often stuff down deep when someone makes us feel as if we're not good enough, but he also points us back to the only One who can truly measure our potential."

> —LYSA TERKEURST, president of Proverbs 31 Ministries
> and *New York Times* best-selling author

"My friend Steven Furtick is one of the most authentic, passionate people I have ever met. His love for God and for people is nothing short of inspiring. He reveals how our tendency to fixate on our failures and major in our mistakes ultimately short-circuits our calling. But even more than that, he points us to a personal relationship with Jesus, the One who calls us, equips us, and carries us into our destiny."

> —JUDAH SMITH, lead pastor of The City Church,
> Seattle, and *New York Times* best-selling author of
> *Jesus Is _____*

"In a world distracted and enamored by external qualifications, Pastor Steven is a refreshing reminder that God looks at the heart. When we respond to him in humility and faith, his power turns even our weaknesses into strengths."

> —CHRISTINE CAINE, evangelist, author, and founder
> of The A21 Campaign

"To watch the ministry of Pastor Steven Furtick is to watch someone living in his grace zone. He is a remarkable communicator, a passionate church builder, and a lover of truth."

—BRIAN HOUSTON, founder and global senior pastor
of Hillsong Church and author of the international
best-selling *Live, Love, Lead*

"Pastor Steven writes books that help us to overcome the lies that hold us back. If you read his words prayerfully and take the truths to heart, God will help you win the battles in your mind and become the person He created you to be."

—CRAIG GROESCHEL, lead pastor, LifeChurch.tv,
Edmond, OK

"Steven Furtick unearths, exposes, and refutes lies and half truths all of us are tempted to believe about ourselves. His direct writing style will keep you engaged. His insights will make you think. But most important, his words will free you to embrace the life God has called you to live."

—ANDY STANLEY, senior pastor, North Point Church,
Alpharetta, GA

"Steven Furtick unlocks powerful stratagems for silencing the inner critic that entangles the believer in a quagmire of self-doubt, fear, and unbelief."

—T. D. JAKES, *New York Times* best-selling author
and bishop of The Potter's House, Dallas, TX

SEVEN-MILE
MIRACLE

JOURNEY INTO THE PRESENCE OF GOD
THROUGH THE LAST WORDS OF JESUS

STEVEN
FURTICK

NEW YORK TIMES BEST-SELLING AUTHOR OF *GREATER*

MULTNOMAH

OTHER BOOKS BY STEVEN FURTICK INCLUDE:

Sun Stand Still

Greater

Crash the Chatterbox

(Un)Qualified

SEVEN-MILE MIRACLE

All Scripture quotations, unless otherwise indicated, are taken from the Holy Bible, New International Version®, NIV®. Copyright © 1973, 1978, 1984, 2011 by Biblica Inc. ® Used by permission. All rights reserved worldwide. Scripture quotations marked (ESV) are taken from the ESV® Bible (the Holy Bible, English Standard Version®). Copyright © 2001 by Crossway, a publishing ministry of Good News Publishers. Used by permission. All rights reserved. Scripture quotations marked (KJV) are taken from the King James Version. Scripture quotations marked (NASB) are taken from the New American Standard Bible®. Copyright © 1960, 1962, 1963, 1968, 1971, 1972, 1973, 1975, 1977, 1995 by The Lockman Foundation. Used by permission. (www.Lockman.org)

Hardcover ISBN 978-1-60142-922-3
eBook ISBN 978-1-60142-923-0

Copyright © 2017 by Steven Furtick

Published in the United States by Multnomah, an imprint of the Crown Publishing Group, a division of Penguin Random House LLC, New York.

MULTNOMAH® and its mountain colophon are registered trademarks of Penguin Random House LLC.

Library of Congress Cataloging-in-Publication Data
Names: Furtick, Steven, author.
Title: Seven-mile miracle : journey into the presence of God through the last words of Jesus / Steven Furtick.
Description: First Edition. | Colorado Springs, Colorado : Multnomah, 2017. | Includes bibliographical references.
Identifiers: LCCN 2016050470 (print) | LCCN 2017001147 (ebook) | ISBN 9781601429223 (hardcover) | ISBN 9781601429230 (electronic)
Subjects: LCSH: Jesus Christ—Words. | Jesus Christ—Example. | Lent—Meditations. | Easter—Meditations.
Classification: LCC BT306 .F87 2017 (print) | LCC BT306 (ebook) | DDC 232.96/35--dc23
LC record available at https://lccn.loc.gov/2016050470

Printed in the United States of America
2017—First Edition

10 9 8 7 6 5 4 3 2 1

SPECIAL SALES
Most Multnomah books are available at special quantity discounts when purchased in bulk by corporations, organizations, and special-interest groups. Custom imprinting or excerpting can also be done to fit special needs. For information, please e-mail special marketscms@penguinrandomhouse.com or call 1-800-603-7051.

Contents

INTRODUCTION

M.O.G.

Easter is kind of like the Super Bowl of Christianity, don't you think?

Our church—Elevation Church in Charlotte, North Carolina —expends a tremendous amount of energy every year around Easter. Countless hours of planning and rehearsal go into preparing for our worship experiences with hundreds of volunteers donating thousands of hours to make it all happen.

Our team goes all out for these services. Original music. Dramatic live elements. Video presentations. Projection mapping. Creative lighting and sound effects. And I try to deliver the most powerful presentation of the gospel message I can. All of this— from the technical elements to the proclamation of truth—is executed with our best efforts. All for the greatest possible purpose—to declare that Jesus is Lord over life and death and that God's grace is greater than our sin and shame.

Sure, I know Easter and Christmas have the reputation of being the times of the year when the "nominal" believers show up at a church service just to keep their Christian membership in good standing. But I think these holidays can also be times when God-seekers dare to venture out of the shadows, hoping to sample something supernatural. What's wrong with that, at least as a start? The spiritually curious are totally welcome at Elevation—at Easter or on any given Sunday. And we've been able to witness thousands of spiritually curious people become seriously devoted followers of Jesus during Easter worship experiences at Elevation.

My wife, Holly, and I and the rest of our original team started Elevation Church with the belief that vast numbers of people in our world are hungry to experience God. Some are far away from him, and they know it, so they're looking for a way to bridge the distance. Others have turned their lives over to Jesus, yet they realize their relationship with God isn't all it could be. It isn't growing. It doesn't measure up to the hopes they had at one time. They know there's got to be more to being in a relationship with God—but how?

More of God. M.O.G. That's what people want—whether they know it or not. Because it's what we all need.

Do you feel that hunger too?

If you do, that's a good thing. That hunger is the starting place of being filled with God's presence. But you don't have to look for God on your own—wandering around aimlessly, frustrated and feeling like a failure. Instead, you can take your first step on a proven path to meeting God and knowing him better and better.

Let me warn you, however, this path isn't an easy one. It's riddled with difficulty and distress. But, if you're willing to take this journey with Jesus as both your companion and your destination, you will experience God's power in ways you didn't even know were possible. And while knowing it's going to be difficult may discourage you, don't let it. Easy isn't what you're called to. On this journey, fulfillment can never be measured in units of convenience and comfort.

This experience begins with both a map and a set of mile markers. First, the map. You've got a seven-mile journey in front of you, my friend.

Resurrected and on the Road Again

Imagine you're Jesus and it's Resurrection Sunday. In the early morning, you have come back to life and left your tomb. To mark the soul-shaking importance of this event, an earthquake has shaken the land. An angel has rolled aside the stone blocking your tomb's entrance, allowing some of your friends to peer in and see that you are gone. Meanwhile, perhaps you wander around the cemetery garden a bit all alone (the flowers smell great after you've been dead for three days!). But soon you show yourself to Mary Magdalene and, a little later, to some of your disciples to let them know the incredible news that you are back.

So far, so good. But what do you do *next*?

Well, if you're Jesus, you go for a walk. The story is told in Luke 24:13–35, and it provides us with our map—a template or pattern, if you will—for our spiritual journey in life.

According to the story, two of Jesus's followers heard early reports about the Resurrection but didn't take them seriously enough to let these reports alter their plans to leave Jerusalem and travel to the nearby town of Emmaus. One of these two followers was a guy named Cleopas. Who was the other one? We don't know because the story doesn't give us his or her name. There's a good chance, though, that this second person was Cleopas's wife. Apparently, they had a house in Emmaus and were going home after spending the Passover holiday in Jerusalem.

Whoever these two were, at one time they'd no doubt had high hopes in Jesus. But after his death, it seemed like the show was over. They were still sure he'd been a great man, an outstanding prophet even, but his death seemed to have put an end to their hopes that he would turn out to be the long-promised Messiah who would rescue Israel. As for the reports that Jesus had risen from the dead, that was just bizarre. Come on, to do that—he'd have to be divine!

These two didn't really get Jesus. And he took their misunderstanding so seriously that he spent a big piece of his first day back from the dead making sure they *did* get him. He'd spent much of his ministry years traveling around Israel with his disciples, teaching them as he went, and now he went on the road again to show these two people who he was.

Another motive for Jesus going to Emmaus with Cleopas and Unnamed Follower #2 probably was that he wanted to keep his people corralled in Jerusalem for the time being.[1] The departure of these two was the first sign that Jesus's squad was starting to scatter. So he wanted to head the travelers off at the pass. He wanted to put them back on the path to knowing him, just as he wants to put us back on the same path when we've begun to stray.

Luke, who narrates this story, informs us that the town of Emmaus was sixty stadia, or about seven miles, from Jerusalem. That makes for about a two-hour walk. Jesus appeared at the side of these two people and asked if he could tag along with them.

Sure. Come along.

The strange thing is, Cleopas and his companion had no idea it was Jesus who joined them on their journey.

Why weren't these two followers of Jesus able to recognize him? Maybe because they weren't expecting to see him. After all, in their minds he was a corpse. Or maybe they didn't recognize him because he looked different after his resurrection. Maybe. But perhaps Jesus actually *prevented them* from recognizing him. Maybe he supernaturally interfered with the facial recognition software running in their brains—because he had a big reveal in store for them shortly.

Let's be clear that Jesus wasn't just messing with the two travelers. He had a reason for concealing his identity. Cleopas and his companion didn't accept Jesus's real identity as the Son of God and Messiah, despite the things they'd heard him say and the miracles they'd seen him perform, and so it fit perfectly that now they didn't recognize his face either. They had eyes but failed to see, as Jesus described spiritual blindness on another occasion.[2]

So Jesus took over the conversation on the road, preaching a walking sermon and using the Hebrew Scriptures to explain that the Messiah had to die and be raised again. He started with Moses and ended with Malachi, putting the Word of God (at least so far as it related to himself) in a new light for them.

As a preacher, I work hard to make sure the truths that I've discovered connect with people in meaningful ways. I love when I see that people are nodding along, shouting amen, or even crying, because these can be indications that God's Word is connecting with their hearts.

I'm in awe of the effect Jesus's preaching had in his two followers because the story tells us that their hearts burned within them while Jesus explained what the Hebrew Scriptures foretold about him.[3] They felt like they were on fire inside! Jesus's words burned up their old preconceived notions about the Messiah and lit a fire of hope and new understanding within them. They were catching on to God's plan to redeem all things through the sacrifice of his Son, and it was amazing!

These two were starting to get the picture of who Jesus really was. But they still didn't connect it all with the man who was talking to them.

At the end of their journey, the two travelers finally did realize who the man walking beside them was. I'm going to tell that part of the story when we get to Mile 7. But for now I want us to think about that journey as the pair gradually came to understand Jesus better, ending in a miraculous vision of the risen Lord. Why's it important to us? *Because this is the journey we need to take in our lives.* Like those two people on the road that day, you and I have got to walk with Jesus, learning from him, observing his ways, and more and more seeing him in his greatness.

We've all got a seven-mile road of our own to travel.

The Jesus Highway

Jesus was a walker. Throughout his ministry years, Jesus gathered his team around him and then crisscrossed the country. Sometimes he headed toward towns and villages where people needed his words and his touch. Sometimes he headed away from people, because he needed to get alone with his Father and pray. Sometimes he stopped by Jerusalem for one of the big religious festivals. Sometimes he had strange appointments in out-of-the-way places that nobody else knew anything about (a woman of low morals in Samaria, a demon-possessed man in Gerasa, for instance).

The disciples had to have wondered how Jesus came up with his itinerary. And maybe Google sync could have helped them get their calendars synchronized with his agenda. But whether or not they understood what was going on at any given time, they went along with him. You see, they knew who they were:

Followers.

Jesus's first words of calling to his disciples were really simple: "Follow me."[4] He wanted them to come along with him and pick things up from him as he went about his business. And so that's what they did. They followed Jesus, both literally and metaphorically, for the duration of his ministry on earth.

Eventually, at the Last Supper, Jesus told the disciples, "Where I am going, you cannot follow now."[5] He was going to the cross alone. So for once these men would have to wait while Jesus went on ahead without them. It must have been disorienting for them.

They were used to following Jesus. They wanted to keep following Jesus. For now, they could only follow so far.

But then Jesus added, "You will follow later." They would rejoin him for a few precious weeks after his resurrection. Then, for the rest of their lives, they would learn to follow his example and leading through the Holy Spirit. In fact, after spreading the word about Jesus far and wide, most of them would become martyrs for his cause. That is, they would follow him all the way to death's door . . . and through it. They would follow him all the way to heaven.

Let me show you why this is all significant for us.

One morning after Jesus was resurrected, he was having breakfast with the disciples—the original Breakfast Club. This was the setting where he and Peter had the legendary conversation in which Jesus said "Do you love me?" three times. After Peter assured Jesus three times that he did love him, and after Jesus told Peter three times to "feed my lambs," Jesus said this to Peter: "Follow me."[6]

At the beginning of their earthly story together, it was "Follow me." At the end it was "Follow me" too. It seems that following was the basic condition for being one of Jesus's people.

And it's not just the original disciples who are Jesus's followers.

When Jesus gave his Great Commission with the word *go,* he turned us all into people who are to navigate the surface of the planet in obedience to his calling. We're never alone in doing this. He's right there by our side. We've got Jesus with us "to the very end of the age."[7]

So we're not just to be *believers*—people who have put our faith in Jesus. We're not just to be *disciples*—pupils who learn from him. We're not just to be *Christians*—those who are known by his name. We're also to be *followers*.

Jesus said, "Whoever wants to be my disciple must deny themselves and take up their cross and follow me."[8] Like sheep who hear the voice of a shepherd we know and trust, we follow him.[9]

Our spiritual journey is not one we take by striking out on our own. We're following in the footsteps of someone else—Jesus. He's our trailblazer. He has gone ahead of us in life as a human being, and he has gone ahead to heaven to prepare a place for us there.[10]

But Jesus is not just our trailblazer; he's also the trail itself!

When Jesus announced he was going away (to heaven), Thomas said to him, "Lord, we don't know where you are going, so how can we know the way?"[11]

Jesus answered, "I am the way."[12] He's a path, a road, a way.

To elaborate, he said, "No one comes to the Father except through me." A journey with Jesus, it turns out, is the only way to truly have more of God.

The apostle Paul understood this. He had a hunger for M.O.G., saying, "I want to know Christ—yes, to know the power of his resurrection and participation in his sufferings, becoming like him in his death, and so, somehow, attaining to the resurrection from the dead."[13] That's exactly what we're doing in *Seven-Mile Miracle:* following Jesus through his death and into his resurrection so that we can be like him.

Paul was totally determined to keep going. He said, "Forgetting what is behind and straining toward what is ahead, I press on toward the goal to win the prize for which God has called me heavenward in Christ Jesus."[14]

Straining forward.

Pressing on.

Reaching toward.

We'll make it to our destination if we keep going and do not stop. The way has already been made.

Famous Last Words

I hate exercising, but I do it because I feel like I'm supposed to. I work out with other people to make sure I keep going. One of the guys I work out with likes to do timed exercises and thinks it's really clever not to tell me how much time we have left on an exercise. He just tells me when we're done.

I told him one day, "From now on, I need you to give me some mile markers, because I need some encouragement when I'm in the middle of the exercise. Tell me, 'Halfway there,' even if I'm not halfway. Lie to me. Just tell me what you need to tell me to keep me going for another rep, because I can't just be doing this and not know how much longer I have left."

Wouldn't it be great if we had a time clock or some mile markers to tell us where we are on our journey with God—and how much further we have to go? To my knowledge, no such definitive measurement of progress exists. But for this seven-mile journey we're beginning together, we're going to mark our miles with the statements Jesus made on the cross.

There's something about people's last words uttered in this life that inspire our curiosity or cause us to treat them as especially weighty. To the law, a dying declaration is testimony that can be admitted as evidence in court cases despite being hearsay. The survivors of an unsolved crime receive comfort if the perpetrator confesses before passing on. Separated family members wonder if the prospect of dying will cause a loved one to agree to reconciliation. Christians hope dying unbelievers will profess a deathbed faith. The disciples of sages and philosophers wait to hear one last pearl of wisdom drop from the lips of the great one who is crossing the boundary of human existence.

Final words recorded in history range from the stirring . . .

- *Patriot Nathan Hale:* "I only regret that I have but one life to give for my country."

To the absurd . . .

- *Humorist W. C. Fields:* "On the whole, I'd rather be in Philadelphia."

To the eerily meaningful . . .

- *Poet Emily Dickinson:* "I must go in; the fog is rising."

To the mundanely characteristic . . .

- *Entrepreneur P. T. Barnum:* "How were the receipts today at Madison Square Garden?"

To the spiritually profound . . .

- *Missionary William Carey:* "When I am gone, speak less of Dr. Carey and more of Dr. Carey's Savior."

Through the miracle of scripture, we have the unique privilege of eavesdropping on Jesus's last words before he died.

It's Good Friday. He's at Calvary, the last stop of his earthly journey. The Son of God and Savior of the world is giving up his life. What is on his mind? What does he want the people standing at the foot of his cross to hear and to repeat, passing it down to the ages?

If you use a red-letter Bible, you won't find much red ink in the accounts of the crucifixion. The Gospels record a mere seven short statements that Jesus made between being nailed to the cross at around nine in the morning and breathing his last breath at about three in the afternoon. Maybe he said more things from the cross that were never recorded for us. But then again, maybe not. Hanging from a cross made breathing—and therefore talking—difficult. Jesus was dealing with terrible physical pain and unique spiritual turmoil, which would have prevented any sort of extended speech. So we can be sure that each of the seven statements he did utter was something important to him, something he cared so much about that he was willing to make the painful effort required to speak it out loud.

From the cross, Jesus voiced three prayers, a promise, a piece of family business, a complaint, and a declaration. These are usually called Jesus's "seven last words," and they have entered deeply into Christian tradition. Preachers since long before my time have preached on these "seven last words." Liturgists have worked them into Good Friday services. Schütz, Haydn, Gounod, Franck, and other composers have set them to music.

They are only seven short statements. That's not many.

Yet in another way, these seven statements are *everything*.

In the Bible, seven is the symbolic number of completion, and Jesus's statements reflect the complete spiritual life, the whole journey of a Jesus follower. Not only do Jesus's last words reveal what was on his mind as he was dying, but they also offer a sequence of the themes that matter most to you and me if we are determined to follow him through life and into the unobstructed presence of God. They're the mile markers on the road to our own personal Easter—not just as an annual event, but as a daily experience.

Here's a preview of these mile markers and what they mean to us: Receiving God's *forgiveness* (Mile 1) leads to *salvation* (Mile 2). When we are saved, we are brought into proper *relationship* with God and the family of Jesus followers (Mile 3). But that doesn't mean the Christian life is easy. As time goes on, we might experience a temporary sense of *abandonment* from God (Mile 4) as well as *distress* in life's circumstances (Mile 5). If we hold on to God, though, we will experience *triumph* through his grace (Mile 6). And the greatest reward will be *reunion* with God in heaven (Mile 7).

The path that Jesus provides isn't the only path in life. There are other spiritual roads, other philosophical paths, any number of routes that our inner GPS might put us on by default. Selfish hedonism, for example, is a wide path that proves popular in every generation. But Jesus's "way" is the only one that will get us where we want to go: to life in the presence of the fullness and the beauty of God. So if we're headed in any other direction, the first thing we need to do is make a turnaround and get on the right road. We've got to repent and receive God's forgiveness. The moment we do, we've arrived at mile marker number one.

The Seven Last Words of Jesus from the Cross

1. *A word of forgiveness:* "Father, forgive them, for they do not know what they are doing" (Luke 23:34).

2. *A word of salvation:* "Truly I tell you, today you will be with me in paradise" (Luke 23:43).

3. *A word of relationship:* "Woman, here is your son. . . . Here is your mother" (John 19:26–27).

4. *A word of abandonment:* "My God, my God, why have you forsaken me?" (Matthew 27:46).

5. *A word of distress:* "I am thirsty" (John 19:28).

6. *A word of triumph:* "It is finished" (John 19:30).

7. *A word of reunion:* "Father, into your hands I commit my spirit" (Luke 23:46).

A WORD OF
FORGIVENESS

"Father, forgive them, for they do not know what they are doing."

—Luke 23:34

The most important thing to remember about the first "word" Jesus spoke from the cross is that he spoke it about us.

Keep in mind, he went to the cross to atone for sins—the sins of everyone who ever lived, including me and you. So we put him up on the cross as surely as anyone in his own day did. And this means he was interceding with the Father on our behalf, asking God to spare us the judgment we deserve.

Jesus seems to have made his first statement almost immediately after being lifted up on the cross, and it couldn't have been what anyone was expecting.

Starting the evening before, he had been . . .

- betrayed by one of his own disciples for money
- arrested by temple soldiers
- interrogated by the high priest Annas
- tried with falsified evidence by the Jewish ruling council
- denied by his most vocal supporter, Peter
- beaten by some temple soldiers
- questioned by the Roman governor, Pontius Pilate
- questioned by the ruler of Galilee, Herod Antipas
- questioned a second time by Pilate
- whipped by some Roman soldiers
- condemned to death by Pilate at the insistence of locals
- mocked by the Roman soldiers and crowned with thorns

- forced to carry his cross to the place of execution
- stripped
- nailed to the cross
- lifted up in the air to hang from his nail-pierced hands and feet until dead

If you were Jesus and you were looking down at the Jewish leaders and their supporters whose schemes had put you there, as well as at the soldiers who had actually carried out the criminal deed, what would you want to say? I won't tell you what I would want to say. It's unprintable.

What Jesus actually said was this: "Father, forgive them, for they do not know what they are doing."[1]

I've always been gripped by the power of that statement. I know that I wouldn't be able to find it in my heart to ask God to forgive the enemies who were responsible for my murderous, scandalous death. Yet the very first thing Jesus did was to issue forgiveness in the face of his betrayers.

He wasn't denying their guilt for their part in his murder, but he was recognizing that they didn't understand the full magnitude of what they were doing. The Jews thought they were getting rid of a blasphemer. The Romans thought they were punishing a criminal. None of them realized they were committing the almost incomprehensible offense of putting to death "the Author of life."[2] So Jesus interceded with the Father on their behalf.

You can't say Jesus didn't practice what he preached.

"Love your enemies," he had taught, "and pray for those who persecute you."[3] That's exactly what he did on the cross.

And that's what he still does today. From his place in heaven, he remains the Great Intercessor.

Think of it in terms of the sacrificial system that played out at the Jerusalem temple. Jesus was like the lambs that were sacrificed. Yet he was also like the high priest who was in charge of offering the sacrifices to atone for sin. That's why the writer of Hebrews said, "There have been many of those priests, since death prevented them from continuing in office; but because Jesus lives forever, he has a permanent priesthood. Therefore he is able to save completely those who come to God through him, because he always lives to intercede for them."[4]

If you are a believer in Jesus, he has interceded with the Father to forgive you. And he continues to live to intercede for sinners. At this moment, all around the world, people are turning in faith to Jesus, and in heaven he is asking the Father to forgive them.[5]

Every spiritual journey starts with realizing we need forgiveness.

QUESTIONS FOR YOU

- *What is your personal definition of forgiveness?*
- *Have you ever prayed to receive God's forgiveness and be saved? If so, when and how? If not, what's holding you back?*

- *When you think of the things you have done that were wrong and that you needed God's forgiveness for, what stands out in your mind, and why?*
- *What unconfessed wrongdoing do you need God's forgiveness for right now?*
- *What are some ways in which other people have forgiven you in the past?*
- *How have you forgiven others in the past?*
- *Whom do you need to forgive right now? For what? How could you go about it?*

MILE 1

Get Your Slate Cleaned Here

A successful journey begins with the end in mind, and so we need to remember that where we're headed in our journey is the presence of God. There, all is holiness, all is purity, all is light.

Like the court of a king where no one will be admitted without proper attire, the presence of God is a place where none of us can go unless we've been cleansed of the stains on our soul. We can't even *begin* our journey until we've been declared righteous, receiving Jesus's pure-white cloak of holiness in place of our rags of sinfulness.

Don't even think about trying to make yourself spiritually pure. It's nonsensical to imagine you could do so, yet that's the way a lot of people think. *If I go to church every week, read my Bible every day, put money in the offering, stop swearing,* avoid gluten, *and have more patience with my kids, God will like me.*

Nothing we could do will ever be enough to get rid of our sin. We just have to receive the forgiveness Jesus offers. We repent, confess, and ask to have our sins washed away. He does the work of purifying us.

When Jesus said, "Father, forgive them, for they know not what they do," his blood was already dripping down the rough wood of his cross. And it still flows today. It covers the stains on our consciences and washes them clean.

Lots of the old hymns I used to sing in church as a kid esteem the cleansing power of Jesus's blood. One, for instance, says:

> There is a fountain filled with blood
> drawn from Emmanuel's veins;
> and sinners plunged beneath that flood
> lose all their guilty stains.[1]

The imagery could make this feel more like a soundtrack to a horror movie, I admit. And the cross of Jesus Christ was nothing if not horrible, and horrifying. But that same cross was the place where the unthinkably horrible became, to us, something beautiful. Scripture says, "The blood of Jesus . . . purifies us from all sin."[2]

Forgiveness may be the first leg of our journey, but it's not something we ever really get past in this life. Whenever we do wrong (and of course we will), we are to again seek forgiveness from God. Whenever others do wrong to us (and of course they will), we are to freely give them our forgiveness, because Jesus has shown us the example.

Made Pure

Annie Lobert grew up in the Midwest with a dad who was filled with stress and anger. As a teenager, Annie took her father's rages personally. She concluded she was unlovable.

A boy she met in high school told her he loved her, and it reached the emotional need that lay deep within her. When he told her he would marry her and make a life with her, she agreed to sleep with him. She was devastated later when she found out that he was also having sex with some of her friends.

Now she had two men she was angry at: her father and her ex-boyfriend.

She moved to Minneapolis after high school, and there she started going to clubs, hoping to meet a rich man who would love her and take care of her. She did meet some wealthy men, but they wanted something else from her than marriage. She began giving sex for money.

"I think what this really was building inside me," Annie says, "was this vendetta, this deep-seated unforgiveness towards my dad, towards the boy in school. And I just wanted revenge. I was going to prove that I could make it in my life. And money was going to be the answer."[3]

Later, she went to Hawaii, where she became a high-priced call girl, earning as much as $2,000 an hour. It seemed like her plan for revenge was working.

One of her clients complimented her, treated her well, and told her that he was falling in love with her. These were the kinds of things she had always longed to hear. So when he asked her to move with him to Las Vegas, she agreed.

But then he changed toward Annie. He started beating her and forcing her to go out on calls with men and give him the money she brought home. For five years she endured abuse from this pimp-boyfriend before finally getting away from him.

But now she was broke. And things went further downhill for her.

She came down with Hodgkin's lymphoma and began receiving treatment for it. Although she eventually recovered from the disease, she became addicted to the painkillers she received for the cancer pain. This led her to cocaine use.

At this time her self-loathing reached a peak. She'd look in the mirror and not recognize the person staring back at her. She would spend hours in the shower trying to scrub herself clean. To no avail.

Although still able to make a lot of money in the "game," she was suffering a kind of post-traumatic stress disorder because of everything she had been through. She couldn't deal with life. She hated who she had become—sex trafficked, used, abused, and an addict.

Finally one night she freebased a dangerous amount of cocaine. The room seemed to go dark before her eyes. She felt a demonic presence with her. Then she had a vision of her own funeral, where her friends and family were crying around her body as it lay in a coffin. In the vision she overheard them say, "She was just a prostitute."

This was the turning point. She knew she needed a fresh start, needed forgiveness. While still suffering the effects of her overdose, she cried out, "Jesus, please save me. I don't know if you're real, but I don't want to die."[4] Soon a peace came over her, and she knew that Jesus had heard her prayer.

Annie had a lot of lingering guilt about what she'd done with her life. She feared that Christians would reject her, and a part of her thought they would be right in doing so. But the Holy Spirit began remaking her heart.

She says, "I started to stand on Jesus's word that I'm whole, that I'm healed, that I'm pure, that I'm a virgin in him."[5]

Annie forgave her father and the other men who had hurt her. She also started the nonprofits Hookers for Jesus and Destiny House to help women like her escape the grip of sex trafficking and pursue a new life by God's design. She had become pure when God graciously forgave her, and she wants others to have the same chance at purity. It's a miraculous opportunity that God holds out to us all.

Coming to God Through the Torn Body of Jesus

I'm getting ahead of myself in a way, but I want to tell you something that happened when Jesus died. This happened after Jesus's seventh "word," but it relates to how we apply his first "word."

When Jesus died, "the curtain of the temple was torn in two from top to bottom."[6] This was a thick curtain of blue, purple, and red linen around sixty feet high. It was quite a feat of the weaver's art and not something that was easily ripped. Yet it *was* torn. And it was torn from *top to bottom*. God put his mighty hands on that curtain and parted it like he parted the Red Sea, making a way for our souls to occupy their Promised Land.

This curtain separated the Most Holy Place—the room in the temple where God's presence dwelled—from the rest of the temple. Only the high priest could go there, and he could go only once a year, on the day of atonement. In other words, the curtain *separated people from God*. Symbolically, God was curtained off. Only the temple system gave hope of getting to him and receiving forgiveness.

Now, though, Jesus is our way to God. We approach God not by a torn curtain but through his body shredded by whips, gouged by thorns, punctured by nails, and pierced with a spear so that blood and water poured out of his side.

His death on the cross is now the means by which people can approach God in repentance, seeking his forgiveness. And we can do this with boldness, not because we deserve forgiveness, but because we have confidence in Jesus's authority and willingness to forgive. There's no reason to hesitate. As the writer of Hebrews says,

> Brothers and sisters, since we have confidence to enter the
> Most Holy Place by the blood of Jesus, by a new and living
> way opened for us through the curtain, that is, his body,
> and since we have a great priest over the house of God, let
> us draw near to God with a sincere heart and with the full

assurance that faith brings, having our hearts sprinkled to cleanse us from a guilty conscience and having our bodies washed with pure water.[7]

If you have never received forgiveness, what's keeping you from crying out to him today? Ask him to forgive you. Place your faith in his sacrifice on the cross. He'll come into your life. He'll resurrect your spirit. The first mile of this journey can be the beginning of a new relationship with God for you.

Consider using this prayer:

> *Father, forgive me of my sin. I know now that I am unworthy to stand in your holy presence unless you cleanse me by the blood of Jesus. So make me new by your free grace. Accept me because of the sacrifice Jesus offered for me on the cross. Amen.*

If you pray a prayer like this "with a sincere heart and with the full assurance that faith brings," as Hebrews says, God *will* forgive you! You *will* begin your journey with Jesus. And it will be a journey paved with grace.

There will be times you fail and make mistakes. The good news is that God's forgiveness doesn't come with an expiration date. It doesn't matter if it's the 1,237th time you've messed up since you prayed the prayer, or if it's the first—you will be just as free to repent and receive God's forgiveness. Forgiveness doesn't just set you on the right road. It keeps you there.

Father, Forgive Them, Even Though
They Know Exactly What They Do

Many of the people who helped crucify Jesus were religious Jews. They thought they were doing God a great service by hanging Jesus up on that tree. In their minds he was a blasphemer because he said he was one with the heavenly Father.

These people were familiar with the same prophecies of the Messiah that Jesus talked about with the followers on the road to Emmaus. The two people on the road felt their hearts burning within them, but the religious leaders had hearts that were cold toward God and led them to participate in murdering the Savior whom God had sent to the world.

It's easy to look down on these people. But what I've recently realized is how much I'm like them. I've gone to church and learned about the Bible since I was a little boy. I've studied Scripture in school and served God in the church. He has shown me time and time again who he is and how I should live. Yet too often my heart is cold and I don't live out what I know.

There are so many things that I know are right to do, yet I don't do them. There are so many things that I know are wrong to do, but I do them. I sin against God over and over again. And every time I sin against him, not only do I shame myself but I also dishonor the Lord who died for me.

I'm not alone in this. Maybe you too have had a lot of exposure to church and know a lot about the Bible but still aren't living wholeheartedly for Jesus.

How many times have you known exactly what God wanted you to do and you didn't do it? Or known the words he wanted you to speak and you didn't speak them? Or known the thing he wanted you to give but you didn't give it?

How many times have you known while you were doing something that it was wrong? Or known that you shouldn't say the hurtful words, but you said them? Or known you shouldn't have gone certain places, but you went there?

So many times when we sin, it's not a lack of knowledge. It's a lack of passion in our hearts.

I believe that Jesus would say about us today, "Father, forgive them, even though they know exactly what they're doing."

The thing to remember is that we don't receive just one delivery of grace. Instead, in Jesus, we receive "grace upon grace."[8]

Of course, the availability and reliability of God's forgiveness is no excuse to keep on sinning.[9] If anything, it's a motivation to change. Why would we deliberately go against a God who is so giving—and so forgiving—toward us?

The thing to do is to keep a sensitive heart, recognize our sin for what it is, and repent immediately. We've got good reasons to be both suspicious about ourselves and confident in Christ. As John Newton, the aging composer of the hymn "Amazing Grace," said, "Although my memory's fading, I remember two things very clearly: I am a great sinner and Christ is a great Savior."[10]

John the apostle said, "If we claim to be without sin, we deceive ourselves." So true. But then he went on with another truth:

"If we confess our sins, he is faithful and just and will forgive us our sins and purify us from all unrighteousness."[11]

Offenses Revisited

There's nothing we can do to earn God's forgiveness. But when we have received his forgiveness, we do have a responsibility. We have to forgive others too.

The forgiveness we receive from God and the forgiveness we give to others are so closely tied together that we can't separate them. Jesus said, "If you forgive other people when they sin against you, your heavenly Father will also forgive you. But if you do not forgive others their sins, your Father will not forgive your sins."[12]

Jesus was not teaching us to forgive people in order to earn our salvation. That would run contrary to the whole theme of the New Testament. Jesus was teaching this: *If you don't give it, you don't 'got it', because if you've got it, you'll give it.* That may not be good grammar, but it's good theology.

When I turned thirty, I felt like God was calling me to fast for thirty days. Reluctantly, I agreed to obey the Lord and began the fast. I don't consider myself the most disciplined person in the world, and I am quite fond of the endorphins released by chewing, so I'll be honest with you—it was challenging.

I started to want to eat things that I normally wouldn't even want. Rice cakes, for example. I dreamed about rice cakes. I would practically have betrayed my best friend for a rice cake. But I persevered.

During the fast, people would ask me, "Are you getting any special visions from the Lord? Like, any kind of crazy revelations from God? Some unbelievable times in worship?"

I'd say, "Besides rice cakes? Not really. I'm having some good times of prayer and reading the Bible, but I can't say that anything breathtaking or earthshaking has happened. I wish I could, but I'm not seeing Philippians 4:19 spelled out in the clouds or anything like that."

The thirty days came and went. I started eating again, and everything seemed right with the world.

Then, about three or four days after the fast ended, I was upstairs in the house where we lived at the time. I had a little room there to pray and read and basically sequester myself from time to time. I was working on a book, and I was feeling happy because my tummy was full of beef jerky.

All of a sudden, God started to deal with me in the area of forgiveness. I felt as if he said to me, *Now that you are on the other side of humbling yourself and surrendering your will to my will, there are some unresolved issues in your heart I want to deal with, because if you don't allow me to deal with these issues, it is going to keep you from progressing to the next level of intimacy with me.* I didn't hear that out loud. As many have said, it was "louder than that." It was a sense within I couldn't shake.

Over the next few days, God surfaced the names of six people in my life with whom there had been an offense in the relationship. In each case, the relationship had ended, and even though I thought several had ended decently well, in my heart there was still a residue of regret or bitterness. I needed to go back, reach out to the person, and make amends.

One by one, I made the phone calls. I sent one or two e-mails. I think I wrote one letter by hand. It depended on what I felt that each particular situation called for. I tried my best to not let it be a self-righteous thing that dredged up old hurts for the other person or implied that they were to blame and in need of my forgiveness. Neither did I try to make each relationship what it used to be. I just tried to make things as right as I could by owning my contribution to the relational pain.

It wasn't easy. I remember my stomach hurting after I made contact with the sixth person on the list. It had been so emotionally draining that it was physically affecting me. For days I was tired.

But in the moments, days, and years that have followed, God released me from some issues of bitterness and unforgiveness. And he has rewarded me with the fruit of many reconciled relationships as well. In fact, as if to put an exclamation mark on this truth, just as I was writing this section my phone rang. I looked down to see that it was the sixth person from my list that day who was calling me! At the time I called him to work out the issue of forgiveness, we hadn't spoken in years. Today he's one of my close friends again—and we've even had the privilege to minister together. (I had to let him go to voice mail so I could finish this chapter, but I love him nonetheless.)

I know God wants you to experience this kind of release and reconciliation too. He wants to break the bondage you might not even know is keeping you stuck and unable to move ahead in your life's journey. I hope you will open your heart to the Spirit of God and feel a fresh wind of freedom like you haven't felt in years.

System 77

One time Peter asked Jesus, "Lord, how many times shall I forgive my brother or sister who sins against me?" Then he made a helpful suggestion: "Up to seven times?"[13]

As we've seen, seven is the biblical number of completion, the number of perfection. And when Peter offered to forgive a jerk who did something lousy to him seven times, he must have thought he was offering all the forgiveness he could be expected to give. In fact, he probably believed he was earning extra credit with Jesus for even suggesting such generosity. Such an overachiever, that Peter.

Jesus said something back to Peter that must have blown his mind: "I tell you, not seven times, but seventy-seven times."[14]

Of course Jesus didn't mean that once somebody has treated you badly for the seventy-eighth time, you're free to break his jaw. The opposite is true. The number Jesus cited—seventy-seven— represents completion to an exponential degree. We have to be willing to forgive without limit.

Jesus didn't want to give Peter a new *standard* for forgiveness. He wanted to give him a whole new *system*. System 77, we'll call it. We're not supposed to try harder to forgive others; we're supposed to take the offense we've received and place it at the foot of the cross, where it belongs.

With System 77, Jesus is saying to you and to me, "There is no limit to how many times I will forgive you, and there is no limit to how many times I can empower you to forgive others. There is no limit to how many times I can heal your broken heart when you're hurt. There is no limit to how free you can be."

To help Peter see why he should be willing to forgive to such an extent, Jesus told a story. It was yet another way he related our forgiveness of others to God's forgiveness of us.

In describing System 77, Jesus began, "The kingdom of heaven is like a king who wanted to settle accounts with his servants. As he began the settlement, a man who owed him ten thousand talents—"[15] Stop right there! Jesus has just started his story, but everybody who was within earshot at this point already knew this wasn't a real event, because a single talent represented twenty years of a working man's wage. And Jesus had referred to a debt of *ten thousand* talents. So Jesus was just throwing out a huge number. It's like a *squillion*. No one would ever be able to borrow ten thousand talents, and no one would ever be able to repay it. Yet only a huge number would do to represent the immensity of our sin debt that Jesus had to atone for.

See, we tend to minimize our guilt. "Oh, my mistakes are not that bad," we say. "Others have done a lot worse." But we don't see what our sin really looks like from the perspective of a perfectly holy and pure God.

Why was Jesus's suffering on the cross so terrible? Why is it such a big deal that he intercedes with the Father to grant us forgiveness? Because our debt is simply enormous.

Now let's return to the parable.

A servant who owes ten thousand talents has come before his master. "Since he was not able to pay, the master ordered that he and his wife and his children and all that he had be sold to repay the debt."[16]

The servant falls on his knees before him. "Be patient with me," he begs, "and I will pay back everything."[17]

Watch what happens next.

"The servant's master took pity on him, canceled the debt and let him go."[18] A debt of a squillion dollars—wiped clean.

When we became followers of Jesus, that's how it went down for you and that's how it went down for me. In a stewardship of justice that seems scandalous on the surface, God canceled our debt and let us go.

What does the guy in the story do next? You would think he would be so happy that he would take everybody out to dinner and pick up the check. But instead he finds another servant, a guy who owes him a hundred denarii.

A denarius was a day's wage. So this debt, while significant, is minuscule compared to the squillion-dollar debt the servant had already been forgiven. This hundred-denarii debt represents the kind of offenses we give to and receive from each other. Things like being cheated, being lied to, being disrespected, and so on. These offenses are real. They matter to us. But stacked next to the mountain of our debt to God, they look like a molehill.

The servant grabs this other guy and begins to choke him. "Pay back what you owe me!" he demands.[19]

So the second servant begs for patience and promises to pay back the debt. In other words, he responds exactly the way the first servant responded when confronted with his debt to the king.[20]

But the first servant refuses this plea for mercy. Instead, he goes off and has the man thrown into prison until he can pay the debt.

When the king hears about all this, he calls the servant in and says to him, "You wicked servant, I canceled all that debt of yours because you begged me to. Shouldn't you have had mercy on your fellow servant just as I had on you?"[21]

In his anger the king turns him over to the jailers to be tortured until he has paid back all he owed. (Isn't it interesting how every time you don't forgive, you're the one who is held captive by that choice?) So it's clear that this story gives us a negative example. It's what System 77 does *not* look like. We are *not* supposed to be like the first servant, receiving forgiveness and then turning around and withholding forgiveness from others. If we do, it's at our own peril. We imprison ourselves.

Offensive Strategy

The Bible tells us, "Forgive as the Lord forgave you."[22] So let me ask you: *Are you giving forgiveness the same way you've received forgiveness? That is, are you giving it freely, generously—not because the other person deserves it—but because it's the right and*

reasonable thing to do? Before you answer, think honestly about
how you've been acting.

When we've been wronged, often we want justice. We want
them to pay. We secretly—or not so secretly—hope they get what
they deserve.

Sometimes I feel that way even when I see somebody zoom
past me and cut me off in traffic. Inside I hope they get pulled over
for speeding. I don't want them to break their collarbone in a crash
or anything, but I would like them to receive a small serving of
justice.

But when *I'm* the one doing the wrong, I don't want justice so
much anymore. I want mercy. I no longer pray for blue lights
when I'm in a hurry.

The first mile of this journey is a mile of forgiveness. The
Savior says, "Forgive them, Father, when they don't know what
they're doing or even when they know exactly what they're doing."
I'm grateful for the complete seventy-seven-times, seven-mile forgiveness of Jesus. He bears with me all the way to that last mile.

Think of all the times when God could have stopped at the
fourth mile, the fifth mile, the sixth mile with you. But he was
patient with you every time. He forgave you.

Is there anyone in your life right now whom you need to forgive? Because here's the truth about forgiveness: if you don't give
it, you might not have fully received—or understood it.

If there's somebody whom you haven't forgiven, if there's
some bitterness that you're holding in your heart about an event,
this is the time at the beginning of your journey to release it to the

Father. Do what I did after my fast. Search your heart for grudges. Pray for God's help to forgive. Make contact with another person to ask for or give forgiveness and to set the relationship right, as far as you're able to. Stop holding past injustice against another person.

It's not easy, but as Anne Lamott says, "Not forgiving is like drinking rat poison and then waiting for the rat to die."[23] In other words, forgiveness is not only a defensive mechanism based on what we deserve, it's also an offensive strategy to win the war against bitterness in our hearts.

Becoming pure like Jesus and entering into the presence of God requires that we lose both our offenses against God and our grudges toward others who have offended us. We can't start moving on our journey until we've been liberated by forgiveness.

A WORD OF
SALVATION

"Today you will be with
me in paradise."

—Luke 23:43

When we see the familiar icon of three crosses in a row, it should remind us that God offers a choice. Like one of the criminals who occupied a cross beside Jesus, we can remain hostile toward God to the end. Or like the other criminal, we can turn to Jesus for mercy. The difference in the outcomes between those two possible choices is as extreme as it could possibly be.

Jesus was one of a small batch of men scheduled to be crucified outside Jerusalem on that spring day. Barabbas, an insurrectionary against Rome, got off.[1] But a couple of thieves were not so lucky. "Two other men, both criminals, were also led out with him to be executed. When they came to the place called the Skull, they crucified him there, along with the criminals—one on his right, the other on his left."[2]

And so the three hung on their crosses in a row on the hill, Jesus in the middle. As Isaiah prophesied, Jesus was "numbered with the transgressors."[3]

Despite Jesus's incredibly merciful prayer for the Father to forgive those responsible for his murder, there was a strange outbreak of malice shortly after he was crucified. It was as if God had taken the leash off the wild dogs, and now the devil had set them barking around the cross. That's the thanks Jesus got for understanding these people's ignorance and asking the Father to forgive them.

Jesus faced a lot of mocking and jeering. But apparently the devil doesn't have much of a sense of humor, because

Jesus's critics at the cross had only one lousy joke among them.[4]

The Jewish rulers standing nearby sneered at him. "He saved others; let him save himself if he is God's Messiah, the Chosen One."[5]

The Roman soldiers copied this jest, putting it in more political than religious terms. They said to Jesus, "If you are the king of the Jews, save yourself."[6]

Even the thieves hanging on either side of Jesus mocked him in the same way. "One of the criminals who hung there hurled insults at him: 'Aren't you the Messiah? Save yourself and us!'"[7] The other criminal joined in with this mockery at first.[8]

These mockers didn't know it, but they presented Jesus with an impossible alternative. Saving himself was the only thing Jesus *couldn't* do, not if he was going to be true to his mission. He came to seek and save the lost—you and me. And he could not save us if he saved himself from the cross. So Jesus kept silent in the face of the injustice and cruelty while the countdown clock to his death continued to tick.

But then something interesting happened. After a while, the second criminal had a change of heart. In fact, he rebuked the first thief, saying, "Don't you fear God ... since you are under the same sentence? We are punished justly, for we are getting what our deeds deserve. But this man has done nothing wrong."[9]

Why did he say this? Perhaps he'd heard the rumors flying around the city during the Passover holiday that Jesus was the Messiah. Maybe he'd even listened from the crowd while Jesus preached. And now maybe something he saw in how Jesus faced death convinced him that—despite all appearances to the contrary—Jesus really was who he'd said he was.

There on his cross, in what should have seemed the most hopeless time of this thief's life, God gave him the gift of faith in his heart. He turned his face toward the center cross and said, "Jesus, remember me when you come into your kingdom."[10]

Jesus gave him assurance—an assurance that incidentally reveals how confident Jesus was in what would happen to him after his death. He said to the repentant thief, "Truly I tell you, today you will be with me in paradise."[11]

Paradise was a term that meant "delight" and was used to refer to the Garden of Eden. So the repentant thief, after a sinful life and a horrible death, was going to a place of delight, where all things are made right. This man was going to heaven.

His earthly journey with Jesus would be over almost as soon as it began. Ours likely has miles yet to go. But just like with the repentant thief, salvation is a crucial stage in our journey.

You see, all of us were enemies of God at one time.[12] We may never have been outright God mockers, but by going our own way and resisting him, we have thrown his grace back in his face. We need the gift of faith to receive salvation and be changed from God's enemies into his friends.

QUESTIONS FOR YOU

- *Would you say that you have received God's salvation? If so, when and how?*

- *What have you been saved from? What have you been saved for?*

- *How has your salvation changed you?*

- *How is God still in the process of changing you today?*

- *What does your salvation mean to you in terms of the choices you make in your daily living?*

- *How do you testify to your salvation before others?*

- *How does your salvation give you hope for the future?*

Ticket to Paradise

When I was in college, I went to China on a mission trip. Most of the locals I met spoke very little English. But they usually had a few English words and phrases they had collected, and they were eager to try them out on me.

One of the things I heard people say over and over again in English was "I remember you long time." I'd go to a stand and buy some noodles, and the woman would study me and say, "I remember you long time." I'd stop into a store to pick up a few postcards to send to my then girlfriend, Holly, and the guy behind the counter would say, "I remember you long time." I'm guessing this is a polite Chinese idiom translated straight into English, sort of like our saying, "I'll never forget you for this."

I knew the people who said "I remember you long time" to me were just meaning to be gracious. But still I thought it was funny. Every time I heard that phrase, I said to myself something like *No, you won't! You don't know who I am. We're never going to see each other again. There are thousands of people* who visit *here, and I'm just one of them.* You won't *remember me a long time.*

I know, I need to lighten up.

But consider this. The repentant thief at Calvary said, "Jesus, remember me."

And Jesus agreed to do just that. When Jesus promised him entrance to paradise, Jesus was not just being polite. He was truly going to remember the thief. And he is truly going to remember us in our moments of need too.

Mile 2 of our spiritual journey into the presence of God follows immediately after Mile 1. Once we repent and are forgiven, we are saved.

Most of us don't go at once to paradise, as the repentant thief did. But like him, when we receive salvation, the spiritual road is opened before us. Our life of following Jesus proceeds to its destination of delight in the presence of God.

Keep in mind that Jesus wasn't just going to remember the thief mentally, as we might suddenly remember someone we went to school with years ago. Jesus was going to remember *and* act on the thief's behalf, becoming his access to paradise. It was a promise that was sure to be fulfilled.

We can trust that Jesus will remember his promise to act on our behalf, too, when we first begin to follow him and every time we need rescue or deliverance of some kind.

1, 2, 3!

The purpose statement of our church goes like this: "We exist so that people far from God will be raised to life in Christ." Presenting the gospel—in the most authentic, creative, and excellent way possible—is what we're all about. We want people to turn to God, receive his forgiveness, and then live in the joy of salvation.

Take the "Raised to Life" weekend we had a couple years ago. We designed the experience to encourage people who had been sitting on the fence about Jesus to make a commitment to him and be baptized right away. I spoke about Peter's sermon at Pentecost and read Acts 2:41: "Those who accepted his message were baptized, and about three thousand were added to their number that day." These people believed in Jesus and were baptized all in a single day.

Finally, I challenged our congregation, "Here's the question: why shouldn't this day be 'that day' for you? When I say three, take your stand with him today. One. Two. Three."

On my count of three, thousands stood up at all our locations. Their action was saying, "I know I've done wrong. I don't want to be one of those people who reject God anymore. Jesus, remember me. Jesus, save me. Jesus, keep me by your side from now on."

We led these new followers of Jesus outside to baptize them as a visible way of expressing the change that had occurred on the inside. It was a beautiful experience. Tears, glowing faces, fist pumps, and other signs of emotion came out when people declared through the obedience of baptism that they now belonged to the kingdom of Christ rather than the kingdom of the world.

In one moment, these people took a bold step of faith and obedience to represent their salvation—a single moment that would change their entire lives. It can happen in an instant, just like the thief on the cross realizing his God-mockery was foolish and turning to Jesus for mercy. It can happen one, two, three.

If you have turned to Jesus for forgiveness (Mile 1), know that your life has changed forever. You have left the kingdom of this world and entered the kingdom of God. You belong to Jesus now. You belong *with* Jesus. He is going to take you with him where he is—into the presence of God. This is salvation. This is the gift of God.

If you have received this gift, Jesus is promising, "You will be with me in paradise." It's absolutely guaranteed.

To help you sense how amazing this is, I want to remind you of a story from the Bible—a story about Joseph. Like me in China, Joseph got a promise of being remembered that he couldn't count on.

Better Late than Forgotten

Joseph was like Jesus in a lot of ways. No, he wasn't a perfect picture of the righteousness of God. But similar to Jesus, he was somebody who honored God throughout his life. Also similar to Jesus, Joseph was a victim of injustice. He was thrown in prison for a crime he didn't commit.

While Joseph was languishing in jail, two servants of Pharaoh—a baker and a cupbearer—were imprisoned with him. That very night, both of these men had strange dreams. They had a sense that these dreams had some kind of predictive meanings, and it disturbed them that they didn't understand their dreams.

"Why do you look so sad today?" Joseph asked them.

"We both had dreams," they answered, "but there is no one to interpret them."

Because he was so close to God, Joseph was good at interpreting dreams. So he said, "Do not interpretations belong to God? Tell me your dreams."[1]

These two guys had some trippy dreams, all full of grapes and bread loaves and stuff. But the dreams weren't too unusual for Joseph to understand, with God's help. The cupbearer's dream meant that in three days he was going to get out of jail and go back to serving the Pharaoh's wine to him. So that was good news. The baker's dream, though, meant that in three days he was going to have his head cut off.

For both men, Joseph's interpretation was exactly how it turned out.

Life for one man, death for the other. Remind you of a couple of thieves on a cross?

Three days for the cupbearer to be released. Remind you of how long a certain dead man had to wait until his resurrection?

This is the kind of thing I love in the Scriptures. It all fits together so beautifully.

But what I want to point out to you most was what Joseph said to the cupbearer: "When all goes well with you, remember me and show me kindness; mention me to Pharaoh and get me out of this prison."[2]

Just like the thief on the cross, Joseph said, "Remember me."

But the Bible says something sad about this. Although this

man got out of prison in three days just as Joseph said he would, "the chief cupbearer . . . did not remember Joseph; he forgot him."[3]

Jesus remembered the repentant thief and brought him to paradise that very day. But the cupbearer forgot Joseph.

Here's how I picture Joseph after the guards let the cupbearer out of the prison. He probably cleaned himself up, collected his few belongings, and said good-bye to his friends in the jail. Then he waited expectantly, presuming the cupbearer's influence would gain him a royal pardon, perhaps that very day. But the pardon didn't come that day. Or the next. As time passed and it became clearer and clearer that the cupbearer wasn't going to be Joseph's means of escape from unjust imprisonment, perhaps he tried to resign himself to living out his days without freedom.

That's how we feel when we need deliverance from problems and situations we seem doomed to face. Our hope burned bright at one time. Now it's just embers.

But if that describes your situation today, think again about Joseph. His story wasn't over.

After some time passed, Pharaoh had a disturbing dream and needed an interpreter. That's when the cupbearer finally remembered Joseph. "Today I am reminded of my shortcomings," he said to Pharaoh.[4] He went on to tell about the Hebrew dream-interpreter. This led to Joseph being released from jail, gaining Pharaoh's trust, and fulfilling his ultimate purpose.

The cupbearer may have forgotten Joseph for a while, but God never did. And he saw that Joseph got the rescue he needed, even if it wasn't quite on the schedule Joseph wanted.

Jesus says to each one of us today, "I won't forget about you. I won't leave you in your prison."

See, just as Joseph told that cupbearer, "In three days you'll be out of here," so Jesus was in effect saying to the thief, "In three days I'll be out of the grave. And believe me, when I'm with my Father, I'll remember you."

And it wasn't just the dying thief he spoke to. He spoke to us too.

Remember that you and I are under the same sentence as these criminals. Our sins deserved full punishment, and we had no hope of getting out. But Jesus remembered us. That's what it means to be saved. It's to be delivered from the dungeon where we deserved to be placed. It's not to be forgotten by God.

This is something we need to keep in mind daily.

Present-Tense Salvation

One thing you hear a lot if you're hanging out with Christians is something like "I got saved at age eight" or "Brother Joe got saved last week." What they're meaning is that somebody started a relationship with God at that time, just like the people who were baptized on the "Raised to Life" weekend I mentioned.

But salvation isn't just something that happens at one point in time. *Boom.* Done. Praise the Lord.

No. Salvation is a process.

Now, it's okay to say "I was saved" if you're careful about what you're talking about. Ephesians 2:8 says, "It is by grace you have been saved, through faith." *Have been saved.* Past tense. That part of salvation is a done deal. You were saved when your sins were forgiven, and that happened in a moment.

But that's not all there is to it. Check out 2 Corinthians 4:16: "Though outwardly we are wasting away, yet inwardly we are being renewed day by day." *Are being renewed.* Present tense. I was saved, but I'm also being saved. There are still some things God is working out inside of me.

That's not even the craziest part. The craziest part is that not only was I saved, and not only am I being saved, but also I look forward to a time at the end of this life when I will be saved. You read this kind of thing in 1 Peter 1:5, which says, "Through faith [we] are shielded by God's power until the coming of the salvation that is ready to be revealed in the last time." *To be revealed.* Future tense.

Salvation is past, present, and future. It's a process.

We understand about processes, right? Lots of things in life are a process.

When your first baby is born, you might think you've "arrived"—because you are officially a parent. But then you find there is endless hard work and heartache still ahead. I hear that it doesn't even quit when the kids finally move out.

A marriage isn't over with the wedding ceremony and honeymoon. You have to learn how to live with each other, day after day, for the rest of your life.

Your relationship with God is a process too. Yes, you're saved. You'll never be more forgiven than you are right now. You'll never be more loved by God than you are right now. You've "arrived" in one sense, but it's going to be a process. It won't be complete until you see Christ face to face and he makes you like he is.

So we don't need Jesus to "remember" us just once—when we first turn to him in faith. We need him to "remember" us over and over again.

We need him to remember us when we're being tempted.

We need him to remember us when life's been hard and we're discouraged.

We need him to remember us when we're fearful.

We need him to remember us when we're confused and don't know what to do.

We need him to remember us when others break our hearts.

We need him to remember us when we have to make decisions.

We need him to remember us when death draws near.

Get used to saying with the repentant thief, "Jesus, remember me."

Reminding God

My kids are brilliant at getting what they want. Not that we give them everything they ask for, but if Holly and I have left the door open to getting them a new pet, or a toy, or a trip to Carowinds amusement park, or whatever it may be, they'll keep asking until they get a definite yes or a definite no. My five-year-old Abbey is especially good at working me with the feminine energy of her smiles and hugs. She has even learned to bat her eyes appealingly. (Are they *born* knowing which buttons to push?)

Jesus told a story about a widow who had been treated unfairly by someone else.[5] She kept bothering a judge about granting her justice. I picture one of the many conversations between the two of them going something like this:

WIDOW: Remember me, Judge?

JUDGE: All too well.

WIDOW: You haven't done anything about my case yet.

JUDGE: I'm busy. I'll get to it.

WIDOW: Why not now? My adversary was in the wrong. I need justice!

JUDGE: I've got better things to do at the moment. You wait your turn with the rest of them.

WIDOW: No, Judge. I need justice now!

The widow was so insistent, the judge was actually afraid she would attack him! In our day, a judge in a situation like that would issue a restraining order to force her to keep her distance. He might threaten her with the bailiff. But this judge gave in and let the widow have what she wanted.

Here's the thing—Jesus wasn't condemning this widow who refused to be put off. He was condoning her persistence, and offering it as an example to be emulated!

We don't have to guess at what this story means for us. The Bible says that Jesus told this story to his disciples "to show them that they should always pray and not give up."[6] We're to be like the persistent widow and keep praying for what we feel we should have. It isn't selfishness. It's a sign of faith.

If you need breakthrough in an area of your life right now, keep going to God in prayer saying, "Remember me, remember me, remember me!"

It's not that God is unaware of your need or that he is indifferent—it's just that he may have a different timing or solution in mind than you do. But still, he invites you to keep coming to him persistently. It shows that you're trusting in him, and him alone, for what you need. It's actually a positive part of your developing relationship with God.

When Jesus had his Last Supper with the disciples, he said to them, "Do this in remembrance of me."[7] In other words, when they celebrated the Passover meal in the future, they were to remember, not only the deliverance of the Hebrews at the Exodus, but even more so the deliverance that Jesus won for all people at the cost of his body and blood. We need to be reminded again and again of his sacrifice. Remembering is so important.

Jesus said to the disciples, "Remember me."

The thief said to Jesus, "Remember me."

We can say to God every day, or even many times a day, "Remember me." Then start living like we believe he's actually going to do it.

A New 24

The prophet Jeremiah, in the middle of a depressing lament, was talking about how the holy city of Jerusalem had been burned to ashes and its people taken into captivity. But he said,

> This I call to mind
> > and therefore I have hope.[8]

In other words, he remembered something.
What did he remember?

> Because of the LORD's great love we are not consumed,
> > for his compassions never fail.
> They are new every morning;
> > great is your faithfulness.[9]

People like the vendors I met in China won't remember you. People like the cupbearer in the Egyptian jail won't remember you. But God will remember you. He will never fail you. He will act on your behalf, time and time and time again. His mercies are new every morning.

I was watching the NBA Finals on TV with my son Graham a few years ago. The game was coming to a pretty climactic close. The difference between the scores of the two teams was only a single point. If the team that was trailing made one more basket in the closing seconds, they could win.

The action was taking place at the trailing team's basket. As the shot clock was about to hit zero, one of the players on that team took a shot. It bounced off the backboard without going through the hoop.

Was their hope for victory over?

No.

A player from the same team grabbed the rebound and took possession of the ball.

That's when the announcer said it: "They got a new twenty-four." He was referring to the twenty-four-second shot clock that had just started over again for this team—and their renewed chance to win the game. But I started thinking about it on a different level, because that's what preachers do.

A new twenty-four. Another chance. Renewed hope.

Isn't that what the mercies of the Lord are for us? They are new every morning, new every twenty-four hours.

Every day when we wake up, we can remind ourselves that God's compassions will not fail. His mercies are renewed with the rising of the sun.

Need some deliverance today? Need a reminder that God has forgiven and saved you?

You've got a new twenty-four. God in heaven remembers you.

A WORD OF
RELATIONSHIP

"Woman, here is your son. . . .
Here is your mother."

—John 19:26–27

W hen Jesus looked down from the cross, he saw many who jeered at him and couldn't wait to watch him draw his last breath. But he also saw some who loved him. This sight inspired his third "word" from the cross.

Even in the midst of his awful physical suffering and the cosmic consequences of his sacrifice, Jesus remembered his family responsibility. He gave instructions making arrangements for one of his disciples to take care of his mom after his death.

This shouldn't be surprising to us. After all, Jesus was all about relationships. He was all about relationships in his earthly life; he's still all about relationships today as he reigns from heaven. That's what makes the third "word" relevant to us.

You'd think all of Jesus's disciples would have been clustered at the base of the cross, wouldn't you? They weren't. Only one of them was present. The others apparently didn't have what it took to be there for Jesus in his last hours.

Like sheep that scatter when the shepherd is struck, the disciples had deserted Jesus when he was arrested on the previous night.[1] Peter denied knowing Jesus.[2] Judas Iscariot, the betrayer, committed suicide.[3] The survivors gathered in a Jerusalem house to hide out behind locked doors.[4] I'm sure they justified their cowardly actions by telling each other, "It won't do Jesus any good if we get ourselves crucified with him."

So, which of Jesus's followers were brave enough to show up for the crucifixion? Mostly women—female relatives of his as well as other women who played a role in his ministry.[5] The gospel of John identifies four of them for us: "Near the cross of Jesus stood his mother, his mother's sister, Mary the wife of Clopas, and Mary Magdalene."[6]

First of all, there might be something about the fact that three out of four were named Mary. But if you set that coincidence aside, this is still a rather interesting little list. We've got . . .

- *Jesus's mother:* She's known to history as Mary of Nazareth.

- *Jesus's mother's sister:* This aunt was probably Salome, the mother of Jesus's disciples James and John.[7]

- *Mary the wife of Clopas:* If Clopas is the same person called Cleopas in Luke 24, then quite possibly here we have the second person who was walking on the road to Emmaus with Jesus after his resurrection.

- *Mary Magdalene:* This third Mary in the bunch was a woman from whom Jesus had cast seven demons and who seems to have become deeply devoted to him as a result. She would soon become the first person to see him in his resurrected form.

Out of these four women, it was Jesus's *mother* that he focused on while hanging from the cross.

When Mary was a girl, she had beautifully submitted to God's choice for her to be the mother of his Son. Apparently a person who felt things deeply, she had pondered the extraordinary circumstances of Jesus's birth and childhood in her heart.[8] She probably worried about him a lot when he became a wandering teacher and was attracting the hatred of the most powerful men in the nation. When he was hung on a cross, it would have been natural for her to wonder whether the plan that had unfolded for her son had gone awry. But she was his mother—she had been there when he was born, and despite the emotional cost to her, she was determined to be there at the end.

Jesus noticed Mary standing below him. He also noticed the one male disciple who had the courage to show up for his execution. In this story, this person is called "the disciple whom Jesus loved."[9] From the context, it is clear that he is John, the man who wrote the only gospel that records Jesus's third "word" from the cross.

Why did he call himself "the disciple whom Jesus loved" instead of simply, you know, John? Probably it was a humility thing. When writing about his own presence in the important events of Jesus's last days and resurrection, he wanted to put the emphasis not on his own identity but on Jesus's gracious favor toward him.

Jesus picked John for an important responsibility. "When Jesus saw his mother there, and the disciple whom he loved standing nearby, he said to her, 'Woman, here is your son,' and to the disciple, 'Here is your mother.' From that time on, this disciple took her into his home."[10]

Apparently Mary's husband, Joseph, had died by this time and Mary had not remarried. As Mary's eldest son, Jesus was most responsible for her now. He could decide whom he would pass that responsibility on to when he died.

The normal thing would have been for Jesus to entrust Mary to his younger brothers. After all, he had four of them, along with at least a couple of sisters.[11] But he didn't do that. Instead, Jesus gave Mary's care over to his disciple John.

One reason for this probably was that Jesus's brothers, at this point, were not believers in him as the Messiah and Son of God. They'd been keeping an eye on his ministry and frankly thought he was out of his mind.[12] The Resurrection would shortly change their minds about him and they would become his followers.[13] But at this time the brothers were at best skeptical about Jesus. So Jesus chose to entrust Mary to the "disciple whom he loved"—John.

Jesus had made a point before about his real family being his spiritual family. Once he rhetorically asked, "Who is my mother, and who are my brothers?" Then he pointed to his disciples and said, "Here are my mother and my brothers. For whoever does the will of my Father in heaven is my brother and sister and mother."[14] So it's not surprising that he gave the responsibility of caring for his mother to his closest spiritual brother, John.

But notice that Jesus didn't merely put John in charge of Mary. He gave Mary a new identity as John's mother. And even though John's actual mother, Salome, was standing right there, Jesus gave John a new identity as Mary's son. Jesus created a new family.

That's what he does all the time for his followers. He makes us a family, with God as our Father and each other as brothers and sisters.

Just as the cross was made of a stake and a crossbeam, Jesus unites his followers on earth with the heavenly Father in a vertical relationship and unites all believers to one another in horizontal relationships. Through his lonely act of self-sacrifice on the cross, he overcame human loneliness and estrangement in a way no one else ever could.

QUESTIONS FOR YOU

- *What does it make you think or feel when you realize that God is your Father and you are his child?*
- *How do you work on keeping your relationship with God open and loving?*
- *Did you know that Jesus calls us his "brothers and sisters" (Hebrews 2:11)? How do you react to the idea that Jesus is your brother?*
- *How has the church acted like a family to you? How has it failed to act like a family?*
- *What could you do to become a better brother or sister to other followers of Jesus?*
- *How has becoming a follower of Jesus made your life relationally richer?*

The Jesus of Nazareth Adoption Agency

I don't do much counseling, but I talk to a lot of people and I hear things. Patterns start to emerge that reveal to me some facts about human nature. One thing I hear over and over is that so many people are deeply, and often secretly, lonely.

- the student who moved from the country to the city to go to college
- the thirty-something man who wants to be married but can't seem to find a mate
- the wife in a marriage drained of the affection it once held
- the teen who just doesn't seem to fit in at school
- newcomers at church who haven't figured out how to get plugged in to the community

I did a little research on loneliness, and what I discovered is that my impression isn't wrong—loneliness is an epidemic. Researchers have determined that at any given time a majority of people don't have others they can talk with when they have something important on their minds. What may be worse is that, in the last major longitudinal study, the number of people who reported being lonely tripled over a period of just twenty years.[1] So this plague is spreading. Fast.

It's deadly too. Did you know that people who are lonely have a 26 percent higher risk of death?[2]

If you think your social media involvement is protecting you from the effects of isolation, think again. There is actually a direct correlation between the amount of time you spend on Facebook and the likelihood that your overall sense of personal satisfaction, including your social connectedness, will go down.[3]

We all long to be in safe, loving relationships with others, don't we? We want to be connected. We want to see and be seen, to know and be known, to hear and be heard.

There's a good reason for that: human beings were designed for relationships from the beginning. In fact, loneliness was the first human problem that God addressed, when he made Eve as a companion for Adam.[4]

But think about this:

- Adam lost some of the flesh and bone from his side when God resolved his need for relationship.
- Jesus took a spear in his side as the coup de grâce to the violence he endured when he took care of our relationship needs.

Jesus's third "word" from the cross was a word of relationship, when he put the mother he was leaving behind in the care of his best friend, John. He understood the importance of people being well related to others, and he took care of it.

Among the other things his death did for us was that it created a spiritual family for us, one we are not born into but are adopted into. As I mentioned earlier, just as Jesus put Mary and John together as a new family, so he puts all his followers together in a new family with God as our Father.

In Miles 1 and 2 of our spiritual journey, we receive God's forgiveness and salvation. Mile 3 is where we are brought into relationship with God and God's people. We should embrace and make the most of these relationships.

Now, I know you might have a hard time believing that God is your Father because of how he is often portrayed. You might expect him to be more like a disapproving judge than a loving dad. Let me reassure you, he loves you and wants to be in relationship with you.

You want more of God. Even more so, he wants more of you.

This Rabbi Is Tough

If you ever feel like God is too hard on you, think about how the disciples must have felt. Jesus was a demanding leader. He was always catching the disciples off guard.

- He told Peter, "Get behind me, Satan!"[5] (It's not exactly a vote of confidence when the Son of God chooses to equate you with the devil.)

- After the disciples asked for an explanation of a simple parable, Jesus exclaimed, "Are you still so dull?"[6]
- When the disciples failed to pull off a miracle, he said, "How long shall I put up with you?"[7]
- Jesus referred to his disciples as "you of little faith" so many times that it was practically his nickname for them.[8]
- Even when he was resurrected and speaking to the two disciples on the road to Emmaus, Jesus said, "How foolish you are, and how slow to believe all that the prophets have spoken!"[9]

These were people he ate with, shared with, walked with, and forgave and loved. But still they were on the receiving end of a lot of hard comments.

Yet I notice that none of the disciples bailed on Jesus because he was too harsh toward them. The one defector, Judas Iscariot, got out because he realized he could make more money if he exercised his free agency option. The others all hung in there with Jesus because they sensed that, despite how he talked to them at times, he loved them.

The rest of Judaism in that era tended to focus on keeping *rules.* The disciples, however, knew they were engaged in a *relationship* with God in the flesh. So, however difficult or disturbing this relationship with the Savior could be on occasion, they wanted it.

I tell you this to assure you that appearances can be deceiving when it comes to having a relationship with God. Even though he may seem tough, that doesn't mean he's any less loving.

Maybe sometimes you read statements in the Bible about how people are sinners, or you come across commands that seem harder than you can handle, and you feel beaten down. How much would change if you started reading God's Word as if he were smiling when he spoke it?

Or maybe you're weighed down with guilt feelings. They may not be appropriate guilt feelings, because sometimes we beat ourselves up more than we should. But then again, it may be legit conviction of sin, the Holy Spirit telling you where you're falling short so that you can repent, learn from it, and do better next time.[10] Here again, remember the love of God and the safety of your relationship with him.

Conviction is totally different from condemnation. We saw in Mile 1 that Jesus is our intercessor. That is, he is like a defense attorney, standing up for us before God. He's not a prosecutor accusing us of guilt. As Paul said, "There is now no condemnation for those who are in Christ Jesus, because through Christ Jesus the law of the Spirit who gives life has set you free from the law of sin and death."[11]

If you hear condemnation coming from the chatterbox in your mind, remind yourself that it's not from your Father above. It's from your Enemy below or confusion within. God wants nothing but life for you.

So when you're feeling like God is too harsh, remember that his disposition toward you is one of favor. He is smiling over you. He loves you and wants to be in relationship with you. Specifically, he wants to be your loving Father.

Abba, Father

Not only does the Spirit of Christ within us not condemn us as spiritual failures, but instead he speaks up to make it clear that we are children of the heavenly Father. Here's how the apostle Paul put it:

> Those who are led by the Spirit of God are the children of God. The Spirit you received does not make you slaves, so that you live in fear again; rather, the Spirit you received brought about your adoption to sonship. And by him we cry, *"Abba,* Father." The Spirit himself testifies with our spirit that we are God's children.[12]

Abba is not just the name of a band from the 1970s. In the language spoken in Israel during the first century, it was a term meaning "father" that expressed affection and trust. Our term that would probably be most similar to *abba* is *daddy* or *papa* when a child refers to a trusted father this way.

Our family relationship with our Creator was God's plan from the beginning. "In love he predestined us for adoption to sonship through Jesus Christ, in accordance with his pleasure and will."[13] Our being God's sons and daughters is what he has always wanted. It gives him joy, just as any normal parent takes joy in having a loving relationship with his or her kids. The cross, bridging the gap between earth and heaven, makes this joy possible.

There's a reason why Jesus referred to God repeatedly as his

"Father" and then in the Lord's Prayer taught us to pray, "Our Father . . ." His Father is now our Father. We're not children of God in the same sense that his only begotten Son is his child. But the heavenly Father adopts us out of love for us. Paul said, "In Christ Jesus you are all children of God through faith."[14]

So no more thinking of God as distant and disapproving. If you are following Jesus, you are in the closest possible relationship with God. He is your Father. You are his son or daughter.

Let me ask you, how's your relationship with your heavenly Abba—your Father? Have you allowed it to be strained by sin you refuse to repent of? Have you let yourself be distracted from it by relationships that you have treated as more important than your relationship with him?

What can you do to increase the intimacy of your relationship with God? It's not a trick question. The obvious answer also happens to be the right one in this case. You pray. You talk to him. It is impossible to have intimacy without conversation.

Jesus prayed often. When he was busy, Jesus prayed.[15] When he had important decisions to make, he prayed.[16] When following the will of God seemed almost too much to bear, he prayed.[17] Three of the seven "words" Jesus spoke from the cross are prayers.

If Jesus needed to pray to the Father, how much more do you? Pray throughout the day. Pray about big things and little things. Pray when you're happy or fearful or bored or in awe. As you pray, you will draw closer to your Father.

I know for some of us prayer isn't easy or even all that appealing. There have been periods in my life when (I'm sorry to say) I've gotten by with short bursts of prayer sprayed heavenward periodi-cally throughout the day, rather than any long, intentional times of intimacy with God. But let me tell you what I've observed about that: a minimal prayer life only holds us up for a while. Before long, we wonder why we're feeling more stress than neces-sary, and we realize what the problem is—our line of communica-tion is down. We sense that there is something basic missing from our lives, something we need, and we recognize that it is heartfelt prayer, the real thing.

That's when we need to return to a pattern of deep and regu-lar prayer. It may feel a little awkward at first, like resuming con-versation with someone we haven't been getting along with well lately. But as we realize the relationship with the Father is still there, we want more and more to talk with him. It feeds a need. Because we love God and he loves us, we talk. That's what dads and their kids do.

But there's more to Jesus's provision for our relationship needs than uniting us with the Father. His service as our adoption inter-mediary goes further than that. He has also enabled us to be ad-opted into his family on earth. As the New Testament says, we are all "members of his household."[18]

Sibs

Did you know that on the night before he died, Jesus had you and me on his mind? It's true. After praying for his disciples, he went on to say to the Father, "I pray also for those who will believe in me through their message, that all of them may be one, Father, just as you are in me and I am in you." He wanted all his followers down through the ages, all who have been transformed by the gospel of grace delivered through the apostles, to "be brought to complete unity."[19]

When you look at the history of Christianity, with its religious wars and its theological mudslinging and its denominational divisions, you have to wonder if this was one of Jesus's prayers that the Father never answered in the affirmative. The external disunity of Christians is regrettable and something we should keep working on. Every family has issues. Yet if we could see things as they really are, on the Spirit-connected level, we'd realize that all followers of Jesus are actually family in Jesus, just as Mary and John became family through Jesus's command.

As the book of Hebrews tells us, "Both the one who makes people holy [that's Jesus] and those who are made holy [that's us] are of the same family. So Jesus is not ashamed to call them brothers and sisters."[20] If we are Jesus's brothers and sisters, then we are siblings to one another as well.[21]

Biblically speaking, the church is the bride of Christ. It is the body of Christ. It is a temple filled with the Holy Spirit. It is also God's family on earth. Acting like a family is how we move toward the unity that Jesus desires for us.

I know a church family can be disappointing, just as a biological family can be. Sometimes *really* disappointing. You've heard

the horror stories of Christian hypocrisy and congregational blow-
ups. So have I. (Maybe we've personally been a part of the horror
stories.) But when a church is functioning as it's supposed to, in all
of its glorious messiness, it's a wonderful thing, a supernatural
thing that no amount of mere neighborliness can match.

One of the single mothers in our church has two young children. One day when her kids were four and six years old, she
became injured when she fell down the stairs at her house while
getting them ready for school. Her doctor told her that for a while
she couldn't drive and she couldn't go to work. Yet she was raising
these kids on her own. How was she going to manage it?

Her small group rallied together. They raised money to cover
her rent while she was out of work. They took her grocery shop-
ping, since she couldn't drive. They helped her clean her home.
They had a game night at her house because sometimes you need
someone to lift your spirits, not just address your circumstances.

This woman had been scared to death about what was going
to happen to her and her family while she was recovering. But
instead of what she feared would happen, she felt cared for and
found that it was a time when God revealed his love to her even
more than before.

God is the one who provides for us, but he does it through the
spiritual family he has placed us in.

We can't be the family of God unless we act like the family of
God. And that means spending time together, letting ourselves be
seen and known and heard, and getting involved in each other's

lives. We're each on a seven-mile journey, but it's a journey we take in company with others, just like Jesus and the two followers caravanning on the way to Emmaus.

I've often said, you have to follow Jesus *for* yourself, but you can't follow him *by* yourself, at least not effectively. Your spiritual success will only be as strong as your support system. So go to church every week. Join a small group. Start serving. Whatever is lacking in your connectedness to the church body God has called you to, see that it gets filled. Conduct your journey toward God together with others.

I know life is crazy. Life is busy. I have a lot of influences pulling me different ways too. But at least one time a week, I'm going to get together with people who are trying to follow Jesus and people who are trying to be people of faith. I know, I'm a preacher. It's my job. But you can do the same. Even if it's not your vocation, it's your privilege and responsibility as a member of the body of Christ to participate.

It may take some sacrifice on your part. But if Jesus could sacrifice his life on the cross to put us together in a family with God and with other Jesus followers, then we can make some sacrifices too. In reality, it would probably be more accurate to describe the sacrifices we need to perfect our unity with other followers of Jesus as mere *changes*. And they're changes we can get used to, embrace, and eventually look back on and wonder why we didn't make them much earlier.

If we recognize our need for relationships with other believers, we'll work to really be family to them and let them be family to us. Unity can begin to develop in the most unpromising relationships.

Taking Down the Flag

One day when I was twelve years old and living in Moncks Corner, South Carolina, I had some trouble with a student at school. When I got home that evening, I told my dad about it. I also mentioned that the student was black.

I'll never forget what he did. He got up and closed the door so we'd be alone. Then he said, "I've been waiting to have this talk with you," and he proceeded to unload the most vile, racist stuff you can imagine, giving me his version of what African Americans are like.

What does not heal gets handed down, and my dad had never been healed of the distorted views of black people he had heard since his own childhood. Now he was passing down to me the hate he had been given when he was young and had kept inside all that time. Jesus said that fathers don't give their children snakes or stones, and they don't normally, but that's what my dad was giving me.[22] It's all he had in his bag.

In a previous book, I told the story about how my dad came to Christ while I was preaching as a college freshman. He had a radical transformation in his life. One way I know this is that he took down the Confederate flag he kept in his barbershop. For years, he would use that flag as a conversation starter when he wanted to tear down black people. But not long after he became a Christ follower, he got rid of the flag. Some of his white customers quit coming to the barbershop, but he let them walk. I thought that was cool. God had intercepted the hate and started turning it into love. But it would be years before I would see the culmination of the change.

Flash forward to June 19, 2011, one of the last Father's Days I would have on earth with my father. (I'll tell you about the circumstances of losing my dad in a future chapter.) This was a Sunday I had planned to take off and go see my dad, who lived a few hours away from me at the time. When we talked that morning, I said, "Dad, whatever you want to do today, we'll do it. Name it."

I thought he was going to suggest that we hit a Chinese buffet. Instead he said, "I want you to take me to church."

That didn't feel so much like a day off for me as a preacher, but whatever. "All right," I said. "What church do you want to go to?"

He said, "Take me to the Bishop's church."

My dad had begun to volunteer a little in a ministry with a bishop who happened to be African American. They had become friends. And now my father, a man who used to think black people were practically subhuman, was choosing to worship in this bishop's church on Father's Day with his son. We were the only white guys in the room. And he was smiling ear to ear as he tried his best to clap on beat.

The Bible says, "There is neither Jew nor Gentile, neither slave nor free, nor is there male and female, for you are all one in Christ Jesus."[23] In the family of God, skin color and cultural background become subject to the God we worship and the love he gives us for one another.

A WORD OF
ABANDONMENT

"My God, my God,
why have you forsaken me?"

—Matthew 27:46

T he fourth "word" that Jesus uttered from the cross has always been the hardest of all the seven sayings for me to
accept. I understand "Father, forgive them." I understand
"Today you will be with me in paradise." And of course I understand Jesus caring for his mother. But in Matthew 27 Jesus
says something that has always disturbed me in a profound
way. After Jesus made sure his earthly mother would not be
abandoned, he had to face abandonment from his heavenly
Father.

Yet what I have discovered upon reflection is that this
fourth "word" from the cross has unique potential for us. It
can bring you and me great comfort about God's presence in
our lives. It tells us that Jesus underwent abandonment by the
Father so that we would never have to.

As we look at this fourth "word," let's get the timing of
events clear in our heads. Jesus hung on the cross for ap-
proximately six hours, starting at around nine in the morning
and going till about three in the afternoon. He seems to have
spoken the first three of his "words" from the cross early during the ordeal. The remaining four seem like they came near
the end, one right after the other.

What's interesting is that the second half of this six-hour
period of suffering was marked by a phenomenon that symbolized how Jesus must have been feeling. The night before,
when allowing himself to be arrested, Jesus had said this was
to be a time when darkness would reign.[1] Now these words

literally came true. "From noon until three in the afternoon darkness came over all the land."[2]

Was this heavy cloud cover? A solar eclipse? Some kind of supernatural phenomenon? Nobody knows.

Whatever caused it, the darkness that lay over the land portrayed what was going on in Jesus's spirit: the son of God felt as if the sun of God's favor had been eclipsed by the sin of the world. We know that by what he said after struggling on the cross for hours and nearing death. "About three in the afternoon Jesus cried out in a loud voice, *'Eli, Eli, lema sabachthani?'* (which means 'My God, my God, why have you forsaken me?')."[3]

Here Jesus was voicing the opening line of Psalm 22. It is a psalm that prophetically expresses much of what the Messiah would experience on the cross, including his hands and feet being pierced, his bones being pulled out of joint, his clothes being gambled for, the mockery he endured, and his thirst. The psalm ends on a note of confidence in God, but it begins with an honest cry of divine abandonment.

Here's where I become troubled about Jesus's "word." It makes sense to me that Jesus was forsaken by Peter. After all, Peter was a rash and fallible man. It makes sense to me, too, that the other disciples would run away. But for Jesus to be forsaken by his Father in the moment of his greatest need? It has always been beyond comprehension to me.

Think about it. After he had been lovingly connected to

the Father throughout eternity, this connection was in some sense suspended and the wrath of God temporarily lay upon him. What would it have felt like for him to suddenly be separated from the Father like this? We can never really know. But we should always be grateful, because Jesus accepted this separation voluntarily for our sakes.

The Old Testament law, when talking about capital punishment cases, says, "Anyone who is hung on a pole is under God's curse."[4] In a truer way than ever before or since, Jesus, while enduring his death sentence, took on the curse of God. As Paul says, "Christ redeemed us from the curse of the law by becoming a curse for us."[5] It was a willing sacrifice.

To understand this better, let's back up a bit and make a comparison.

At the beginning of his ministry, Jesus had submitted to a baptism of repentance. He didn't need to repent. He was sinless. Instead, he was baptized to identify with sinners like you and me. John the Baptist sensed this, because he called Jesus the sacrificial Lamb of God.[6]

And now, at the end of Jesus's ministry, he submitted to a death he didn't deserve. It's not a coincidence that his death occurred at 3 p.m., the same time of day when the Passover Lamb was slaughtered at the temple. Jesus gave his life as a ransom for many.[7] "Christ, our Passover lamb, has been sacrificed."[8]

At the baptism, Jesus heard the affirmation that the Father was well pleased with his Son. On the cross, by contrast, the Father turned his back on the Son. But it was all part of the same process of Jesus providing a sacrifice for our sins.

On Mount Calvary, Jesus was experiencing the consequences of his own decision to give himself up. To become the sacrificial Lamb, he had to take our sin on himself.[9] Paul said, "God made him who had no sin to be sin for us, so that in him we might become the righteousness of God."[10] That's why Jesus agreed to be estranged from the Father for a while—to make us holy and acceptable to God.

It's safe to say that the greatest pain Jesus endured had nothing to do with whips and thorns or nails and asphyxiation. As awful as all that was, the worst aspect of the crucifixion for Jesus was going through separation from his Father. But because Jesus was willing to do this, you and I can rest assured that we never have to be separated from our heavenly Father for one moment in our lives. No matter what trials or storms the devil brings our way, we'll never have to wonder if our Father has forsaken us.

QUESTIONS FOR YOU

- *Since becoming a follower of Jesus, have you ever felt as if God were hiding his presence from you? If so, what was the hardest part of that for you? What questions or doubts did it raise in your mind?*

- *If you have ever felt as if God withdrew his presence from you, has the feeling gone away yet? What caused the cloud to lift?*

- *Have you ever gone through depression? What was it like? What questions did it raise about your faith and relationship with God?*

- *What Bible promises or theological truths could you cling to as a reminder that God will never truly depart from you?*

- *What things help you to maintain faith and hope as a follower of Jesus over the long term?*

Godforsaken

Ten years after Mother Teresa died, a friend of hers published a collection of her letters and other writings. The book is called *Come Be My Light,* and it quickly became a bestseller.

What do you think the media seized on for their news bytes about the book? More than one journalist suggested that because the book revealed that for many years Teresa didn't feel like God was present in her life, she might not have been a believer in God at all.

No, no, no.

Saint Teresa of Calcutta was going through a spiritual experience that saints have long recognized and have called a *dark night of the soul.* (Not to be confused with the "Dark Knight.") The dark night of the soul is a time when a believer feels separated from God but really isn't. It's a kind of spiritual depression with a major component of loneliness.

It's true that shortly after Teresa began her work among the poor and dying in Calcutta, she began to sense the absence of Jesus. Her term for her feelings of loneliness and abandonment was "darkness." The experience was intensely painful for her.

At one point, Teresa wrote:

Darkness is such that I really do not see—neither with
my mind nor with my reason—the place of God in
my soul is blank.—There is no God in me—when
the pain of longing is so great—I just long & long for
God—and then it is that I feel—He does not want
me—He is not there. . . . The torture and pain I can't
explain.[1]

Eventually a spiritual adviser helped Teresa see that her sense
of abandonment by God actually had a benefit for her work: it
helped her better understand the people whom she was serving.
Also, she began to identify her painful sense of spiritual abandonment with the suffering of Jesus. All this helped her to accept her
"darkness" and keep going in faithfulness to God despite it.

Apparently the Roman Catholic Church didn't agree with the
journalists' interpretations of Mother Teresa's struggles. They officially designated her a saint in September 2016.

It hurts when you want more of God but instead it seems like
you get less of him. But if you ever go through a period of time
when it feels as if God has abandoned you, don't let it drive you to
despair. If Jesus and Mother Teresa went through it, why not you?
Easter is proof that you can *know* that God is with you, even if
you don't *feel* his presence all the time, and in faith you can act
accordingly.

Where the Journey Becomes Rocky

This is Mile 4 of your spiritual journey, the halfway point. Some time has passed since you began walking with God. These aren't the early days of asking for forgiveness, being saved, and joining God's family. It's a time in your life when you're reaching spiritual maturity. And God is now allowing you to experience some harder stuff.

A dark night of the soul doesn't usually come to new followers of Jesus. It comes to those who are more experienced in the faith, even if not quite as experienced as Mother Teresa. So if you have a sense of abandonment, then maybe in a strange way you can take it as a vote of confidence from God. He's letting you go through it because he knows you can handle it, with the help of his Word, his Spirit, and his people around you. It doesn't make it less painful, but pain is more bearable when it serves a greater purpose.

Now, there is such a thing as having a disruption in your relationship with God because you have sinned. The solution in a case like that is obvious: remember what you learned from Mile 1 of your journey. Repent and receive God's forgiveness. Then get back on track.

But what we're talking about here is having a sense of being estranged from God even though you *haven't* done anything to cause it. Jesus had done nothing to deserve having been forsaken by God on the cross. And sometimes we might feel abandoned by

God, too, through no fault of our own. We can't just move on from it by putting out extra effort.

I know you may not feel estranged from God *right now.* And in fact you might not *ever* feel that way. If so, I'm happy for you. But I hope you'll keep reading this chapter anyway, because I think likely someday you *will* have your own dark night of the soul, maybe more than once. Or somebody you care about may go through the experience. This chapter is to help prepare us for that possibility.

I also want to encourage you with the truth that if God is letting you go through a time of feeling separated from him, you can be *absolutely sure* that it has a part to play in his good plan. God is not emotionally abusive. There's a reason for everything he does—and everything he allows.

If you are going through a dark night of the soul, ask yourself, *Why is God allowing me to go through this?* I can't tell you the reason for certain, but I can make some guesses.

Maybe he's using it to exercise the muscles of your faith. If you keep trusting and being obedient even while God seems out of sight, you'll come out on the other side of this dark night stronger than ever.

Maybe God wants you to focus on *knowing* him better rather than *doing* things for him, or him doing things for you. Sometimes a sense of distance can drive you to desperately seek God's face.

Maybe, as in Mother Teresa's case, God is using this experience to make you better able to understand and serve other people who are far from him.

Or maybe there's a reason that is beyond what we can even guess. You might have to wait until paradise for the explanation.

In the meantime, one thing is clear. If you are feeling as though God has withdrawn, he hasn't. And there *will* come a time when he will reveal himself again. And when that happens, you'll be a person who has a more fully developed sense of who God is and who you are in relation to him.

Even though it may seem that you cannot hear from God right now, he is saying to you, "I will make you fruitful in your frustration." He is promising, "You're going to lose count of all the ways I'm going to bless you if you'll submit to the mystery of my will in this season."

Hold on to the invisible God.

Under Pressure

Jesus knew ahead of time what he was going to suffer on the cross and, humanly, he dreaded it. His horror at what he faced rose up and overwhelmed him when he prayed in the Garden of Gethsemane on the night he was arrested. He was in such anguish that his sweat became like drops of blood.[2]

Honestly, this scene in the garden isn't easy for us to read about, much less for Jesus to actually have gone through. But if we want to understand our Savior and follow in his footsteps, we've got to face it.

My wife hates watching scary movies. Also, what I consider almost a comedy, she categorizes as scary. She also happens to be very jumpy and grabs me during every scary scene. I rather enjoyed this when we were dating, but for some reason, it's lost its charm after fifteen years of marriage.

Holly will look at me in those moments of dramatic tension and ask, "Can we please skip this scene?"

My response is always the same. "No, 'cause this is the scene that's going to set up the rest."

The scene in the Garden of Gethsemane sets up the scene on the cross and the Resurrection that follows.

As Jesus prayed in the garden and sweat drops of blood, I think he must have been anticipating the abandonment of all of those who had promised they would go to death with him, those he had fed and cared for and taught. But more than that, he must have been anticipating the greatest moment of agony that anyone could ever experience—separation from the source of life, God himself.

In the garden, Jesus prayed, "My Father, if it is possible, may this cup be taken from me."[3] In other words, *I don't want to be abandoned. I don't want to be separated from you. Not even for a moment.*

But he also said something else that you and I need to get in our spirits as we continue this journey: "Yet not as I will, but as you will."[4]

Our will would be to never go through suffering or feel as if God were far away. His will might be to lead us through dark seasons when we have to grope our way forward by faith. And this is when we have to make a call: Will we trust his will, or will we waste our time whining in an attempt to get our own way?

The name *Gethsemane,* the hillside where Jesus often went to pray, means "olive press."[5] I think it's significant that the Bible says Jesus prayed in the place of the olive press, because the only way you can get oil from an olive is to press the olive. The anointing of God is only produced under pressure.

There's a great word of application here as we think about our own experience of apparent forsakenness. If we trust God, he'll take us through this valley of the shadow of death, and the green pastures on the other side will be worth whatever we've gone through. We need fear no evil because—despite all appearances to the contrary—our heavenly Shepherd really is with us.[6]

A Matter of Perspective

I was talking to someone who grew up largely without a father. His father was abusive to him in his early years, and then the father died. I asked him, "How do you think it affected you to be abandoned by your father?"

He started to share with me how it affected his confidence, how it affected his sense of ability to love other people, how he has all these fears about whether he will be a good dad to his kids. The consequences of fatherlessness for this guy were pretty harsh.

As he went on and on, I was thinking, *What kind of father abandons his son?*

I've got two sons and a daughter, and I can't imagine abandoning them. When I do have to leave them temporarily, I want to hurry back.

A few years ago I had a memorable experience returning home from a preaching trip. My team and I had taken a small plane that someone in our church let us use.

On the way back, there was a storm in front of us. Because our plane was so small, we had to fly around it. So instead of leaving at 8 p.m. and getting home before midnight, as we'd planned, the trip took around ten hours. We flew all night, stopping five or six times for fuel.

It was unforgettably excruciating. I felt like an eight-year-old when I kept asking the pilot, "Are we there yet? Are we there yet?"

Finally, about 7:30 in the morning, I walked into my house. My son Graham—who was probably five years old at the time— came running up to me for a hug.

Then he asked me a ridiculous question.

"Daddy, how'd you get home so quick?"

Are you kidding me? How did I get home so quick? I've been flying all night! But all he knew was that he went to bed, woke up, and here came Daddy through the door. "How'd you get home so quick?"

To me, my absence from home seemed endless. To Graham, it seemed like I was hardly gone at all. It was a matter of perspective.

We need to have the right perspective on our sense of absence from God as well. Perception: God is absent. Reality: he's right there all along.

Let me repeat that: *If you are a child of God, then no matter how abandoned or lonely you may feel, God has been with you and he's with you right now.*

You see, when we come to God, we come through the way that Jesus has already made. We come through the way of the cross. We don't have to sweat drops of blood in a garden; he's already sweat those drops for us. We don't have to feel spikes going through our feet and hands because he's already endured that pain. And we don't have to be separated from God either. Not now. Not ever.

Jesus experienced abandonment from his Father so that we never have to. Because he was forsaken, we never have to be.

We come to God in salvation, and it's almost like we think, *That felt too easy.* We think we should have to earn it. We feel like we ought to keep some rules. But that's not the way it works. Jesus took God's punishment on himself so that we wouldn't have to. There's nothing we can add to what he's done.

You may *feel* forsaken, but you're never forsaken. You and I can never truthfully cry what Jesus cried: "My God, my God, why have you forsaken me?" Because that same Jesus who was forsaken says to us, "Never will I leave you; never will I forsake you."[7]

Jesus didn't fly all night on an airplane to go from one city to another. He left the glories of heaven, came to Earth, and was abandoned by the Father for our sake. I love the worship song we used to sing in the early 2000s that says, "I'm forgiven because you were forsaken."[8]

There's something else I want to say about this: even the *appearance* of being separated from God is only for a moment, if you look at the big picture.

God with Us

When Jesus came to earth, his name was called Immanuel, meaning "God with us."[9] If you go to the last book of the New Testament, it says that he is the one "who is, and who was, and who is to come."[10] So from the time that Jesus came to earth in the form of an infant to the time when he reigns in heaven, we know him as the ever-present God.

On the night before he died, Jesus said to his disciples, "I will not leave you as orphans."[11] That's what a sense of estrangement feels like, doesn't it? We feel orphaned. But once God has adopted us as his children (as we learned in the last mile), he never gives us up.

Jesus added in his assurance to the disciples, "I will come to you." He knew good and well that very soon, on the cross, his own Father would not come to him. God the Father had to leave Jesus on the cross as the payment for our sins. He had to let him die all alone. Yet Jesus will come to us. In the body, he temporarily parted from the disciples, but spiritually speaking, he never really leaves any of his followers.

And Jesus shows us something in his moment of abandonment, his moment of deepest despair, that I think you and I can carry with us for the rest of our lives. See, it's only for a moment. That's why Paul said that "our light and momentary troubles are achieving for us an eternal glory that far outweighs them all."[12] It's only for a moment when you feel alone and abandoned.

Jesus was abandoned by the Father for just a few hours. Mother Teresa felt that way for several years. Many other people feel separated from God for a season of life. However long the experience drags out though, in the perspective of eternity those feelings last for just moments. They're nothing compared to the reality that God is, was, and will eternally be with us. He's always there.

In an earlier chapter, I mentioned how Joseph (from the book of Genesis) was thrown into prison. Like Jesus, he hadn't done anything to deserve this kind of treatment. But still, there he was, languishing behind bars.

In this situation Joseph must have felt abandoned by God, forsaken. But the Bible says this: "While Joseph was there in the prison, the LORD was with him."[13]

The Lord was with him.

The Lord is with you too in whatever "prison" you feel yourself incarcerated in.

If you'll look back over your life, I bet you could find some evidence that God was with you even when you were going through things you didn't want to go through. He was with you even through the divorce. He was with you even through the abortion. He was with you even through the bankruptcy. He was with you even through the failure, the loneliness, or the betrayal.

I'm grateful that I can look back over my life and realize that, though some people who said they were my friends left me, God has never left me. He's with me today. He's with you today as well. And he'll never leave us. For you and for me, he's "a friend who sticks closer than a brother."[14]

Believe in the Bubble

On my iPhone, the texting app is called iMessage. I use it all day and half the night sometimes, it seems like. But what I find interesting is that it's got this thing called the *typing awareness indicator.* That's the technical name for it. I call it, and other people call it "the bubble."

Here's the way it works. You text something. Then while you're waiting, you see something pop up that looks like a dialogue balloon in a cartoon, and inside it are three dots scrolling. That's "the bubble." It tells you that the person you're texting with is writing something back to you. You just need to wait until the other person is done, and you'll see the response in your dialogue.

Sometimes you'll send an important message to someone, and here comes the bubble. The bubble will be up there on and off for, like, five minutes. You're thinking, *Oh, they're typing something deep.* If you're dating somebody, you're thinking, *Maybe he's typing me a poem.* Or, *she's telling* me *how she really feels about me, finally.* You can't wait to find out what it is.

An important thing to remember about these bubbles is that the other person can see when you're typing too.

One time a guy texted me a question. I wanted to take my time responding to him because I wasn't sure what I was going to say. So I typed a little, then stopped. Then typed a little more and stopped again. All without sending my message. Maybe a minute passed while I was still thinking about what I wanted to say.

That's when this guy texts me back and says, "I know you're there. I see your bubbles." Can you say creepy?

This might be a silly illustration for something so serious, but sometimes it seems like you're waiting and waiting for God to reply to your request. I mean, you've prayed—you've begged him to do something for you or show himself to you—and what comes back? Nothing. Did he take another call? Did he put down his iPhone to get a snack? Is the signal weak in that part of heaven?

We've got to learn to trust God . . . even when all we see is bubbles.

What to Do While You're Waiting for the Sun to Come Out Again

I don't know exactly what you're going through if you're struggling with a sense of separation from God, but I do know some steps you could take that have helped others in a similar situation.

Take a deep breath and don't panic. What you're going through isn't unusual and it isn't permanent. You'll get through this.

Remind yourself as often as necessary that your feelings aren't always reliable guides. God is there even when you don't sense his presence. Truth trumps emotion.

Recall past times when you felt God's intimate presence. You may not be feeling the same way now, but God's love for you hasn't changed a bit.

Hold on to the promises of Scripture. God has promised us his presence forever. Remember the power in verses like "Never will I leave you; never will I forsake you."

Keep on taking care of your physical and mental health. If you don't, you could be making your experience of a dark night of the soul worse than it has to be.

Keep on being faithful to God. During the dark night, you could be vulnerable to temptations to stop obeying God, since it seems like he isn't interested in you anymore. Don't let the devil take advantage of you in a vulnerable time. Hold fast.

Focus on maintaining your side of your relationship with God. Keep reading your Bible. Keep praying. Keep going to church, worshiping, and connecting with your spiritual family, who can reassure you of God's love.

Look for what you can learn from the experience. A lesson is there and will become plainer over time.

Be patient. The experience is momentary, remember?

Before I leave this subject, I want to assure you one more time of how desperately God loves you and values his relationship with you.

Never Underestimate a Father's Love

As you may notice, I get some of my best illustrations from airplanes and airports. I took my oldest child, Elijah, on a preaching trip (to Louisiana!) for the first time when he was five years old. It was a last-minute decision that I made simply because he randomly asked to come. What I didn't think about when I agreed to his coming along is that I would have to take him through the airport without Holly, who wasn't going with me on this trip. Sounds simple enough. But nothing is simple when airport security is involved.

So I'm going through airport security, which is already dehumanizing and nerve-wracking. You know how they strip you and mock you and beat you and spit upon you. I get more sympathy for what Jesus went through on the cross every time I go through. But this time, I have my five-year-old with me, which intensifies my stress.

Suddenly, a rude young TSA guy walks up to me and says, "Excuse me, sir. I need your son to come with me."

I say, "That's fine, but we should come through together because he's five."

He says, "No, your son needs to go through with me right now, and then you can come through after."

I don't like that very much, but I figured, *Let's just get this over with.* This guy's *a* trained *professional.*

But somehow, Elijah and the TSA agent disappear from my sight at the same time the line stops and they won't let anyone else through. Now I'm stuck on the other side of the metal detectors, trying unsuccessfully to get a visual on my son.

I try to get somebody's attention. At first I try to do it in a dignified way, but I notice it's getting me nowhere. Time to escalate. I know there are probably some church members in the Charlotte airport who know who I am, but I really don't care at this moment. I might be a pastor, but right now I'm a daddy, and I feel the spirit of Liam Neeson in the movie *Taken* coming upon me with a vengeance. So I take a slightly less religious approach, colorfully and loudly trying to explain that they need to let me through to be with my son . . . right now . . . or else.

A man in a uniform comes over to advise me. "You need to calm down, sir."

I offer some counter advice. "No, *you* need to calm down and let me be back with my son. I can't see my son, and I don't LIKE it."

He tries to assure me that if I'll just calm down, I'll be with my son in a minute.

I explain that they told me that a few minutes ago, and I *was* calm, but I can't be calm anymore because my internal calmness clock has expired. I said it a little differently than that, and then I began the process of letting myself through security without permission. At this point I hear the TSA announcement over the intercom (that apparently addressed the entire airport):

"We've got a Code 1! We've got a Code 1!"

I assume that Code 1 doesn't mean VIP passenger in need of assistance.

After a few minutes of threats (from both parties) and chaos, the TSA supervisor comes over to apologize. "Sir, I'm so sorry. They should have never separated you and your son. That agent will be disciplined. I'm so sorry."

Finally, someone with some sense. I start to cool off. A little bit.

Still shaking with adrenaline, when I finally get through and find Elijah, I am disappointed by his disposition. He's supposed to be melting down so I can scoop him up in my firm fatherly embrace and assure him everything is all right. But he's not upset. He's in complete chill mode. Looking rather unbothered and oblivious.

Once we got on the plane, I brought it up.

"Son, I'm curious. They separated us. Why weren't you crying or freaking out?"

What he said next was perfect. I could not have scripted it any better to illustrate my point.

He said, "I could hear your voice the whole time. I knew you were coming."

Wow.

"Plus, I was thinking about Mario Kart," he added.

The confidence of a follower of Jesus is the confidence of a child who knows: my Father is close. And he's coming. I can hear his voice. Even in the darkness.

A WORD OF
DISTRESS

"I am thirsty."

—John 19:28

After his dramatic statement of his sense of abandonment by the Father, Jesus next said something seemingly ordinary: "I am thirsty."[1]

In this fifth "word" on the cross, Jesus was speaking out of his humanity. After the torture he had experienced, after the copious bleeding, after exposure on the cross for hours, he must have been horribly dehydrated. He needed fluid.

Written centuries earlier, Psalm 22 vividly pictured this part of Jesus's suffering:

> My mouth is dried up like a potsherd,
>> and my tongue sticks to the roof of my mouth;
> you lay me in the dust of death.[2]

"I am thirsty" may be the easiest of all the seven "words" for us to relate to. We all know what it's like to be thirsty. We all know what it's like to have human distresses of many kinds—hunger, sickness, injury, pain, loneliness, fear, depression, disappointment, and so much more.

Jesus understands. He's been there. As Hebrews says about him, "Since the children have flesh and blood, he too shared in their humanity."[3]

But Jesus's fifth "word" was more than just a bare statement of his physical need. It had a deeper level to it. Remember, he had been feeling abandoned by the Father. So on the spiritual level, he was thirsty for a return of the living water of God's presence.

This is also something we can relate to. We, too, repeatedly find ourselves longing for more and more of God. In fact, at one and the same time we might thirst for what we lack physically and thirst for what we lack spiritually.

If anything that could be called comical occurred during the crucifixion, it came at this point.

As you remember, Jesus had just cried out, *"Eli, Eli, lema sabachthani?"* He was quoting the first line of Psalm 22 in his local language, crying out, "My God, my God, why have you forsaken me?" But some of the people who were listening misunderstood what he'd said. *"Eli"?* they thought. *Maybe this supposed Messiah is calling out for the prophet Elijah to come and save him. Let's see what else he'll say.* So someone ran to soak a sponge in wine vinegar and put it on a staff.[4]

Even this *ridiculous* misunderstanding played into Jesus's hands.

Keep in mind that while the entire crucifixion seemed to onlookers like something that was done to Jesus, it was actually something that *Jesus chose to do.* And we see that proved here. Jesus had a specific reason for wanting someone to bring him a drink at this point: "Knowing that everything had now been finished, and so that Scripture would be fulfilled, Jesus said, 'I am thirsty.'"[5]

Already, Jesus had fulfilled many prophecies of the Messiah on the cross. Now he knew he was about to die, and there was one more prophecy he wanted to fulfill first. Psalm 69:21

says, "They put gall in my food and gave me vinegar for my thirst." Jesus needed to drink vinegar.

Meanwhile, there was probably another, more practical reason for Jesus wanting something to drink. He had two more "words" to say—two important statements to make, which we will be getting to in Miles 6 and 7. He wanted to shout them out in a voice that everyone could hear, and so he probably wanted to wet his throat in preparation.

Six hours earlier, when Jesus had arrived at Golgotha and was about to be nailed to the cross, the soldiers had offered him wine mixed with myrrh. This drink would have dulled his pain. *Most of us* would have taken it. But Jesus refused the anesthetic drink.[6] For our sake, he was going to fully experience the suffering that was to come.

With the end drawing near, however, he was now prepared to accept a drink, and he got it. "A jar of wine vinegar was there, so they soaked a sponge in it, put the sponge on a stalk of the hyssop plant, and lifted it to Jesus' lips."[7]

The passing mention of hyssop—a tall, flowering herb—is more significant than it might seem at first to us. It would have resonated immediately in the minds of anybody familiar with the Hebrew Scriptures. Back at the time of the Exodus, the Hebrews had used stalks of hyssop to paint lambs' blood on their doorposts as a sign for the angel of the Lord to pass over them.[8] Now Jesus the Passover Lamb was being slain. The law also said that hyssop was to be used to spatter blood as a sign of purification for a diseased person or an infected house.[9]

David therefore prayed metaphorically, "Cleanse me with hyssop, and I will be clean."[10] Because of his shed blood, Jesus cleanses all who repent. So at Calvary a stalk of hyssop not so coincidentally served to raise a sponge up to the level of Jesus's lips.

This sponge was saturated with vinegary wine, a cheap but refreshing drink that the soldiers had probably been chugging down as the hours of the crucifixion slowly passed. It was a bitter vintage. But then, the whole experience had been bitter for Jesus. That day, Jesus drank the cup of God's wrath to the dregs so we would never have to taste it.

"I am thirsty" may seem a mundane statement. But it gives us hope that God will *quench* our thirst for the needs we have in this life. Especially for our need to experience more of him.

QUESTIONS FOR YOU

- *What kinds of distress are you experiencing in your health?*
- *What kinds of distress are you experiencing in your relationships?*
- *What kinds of distress are you experiencing in your finances or career or life goals?*
- *How has your distress affected your faith? And how has your faith affected your distress?*
- *What lessons or growth opportunities might God have for you in the midst of your distress?*

- *How is God using your distress to draw you to himself?*
- *What reasons do you have for hope about your distresses?*

MILE 5

Parched

In 2014 my dad died of ALS, also known as Lou Gehrig's disease. What the disease did to his body is very difficult to describe if you have not personally witnessed it.

What it did to his relationships was even worse. A pattern of my dad's verbal abuse and threats toward my mom resulted in my dad leaving my mom, and living on his own, for a period of months. He refused all of our attempts to arrange a place for him to live close by so we could help care for him. And when we would pay for someone to come and care for him, he would find a reason to fire them every time. These dark months included repeated threats from my dad toward us and himself—and a downward spiral that made me wonder whether we might end up killing him before the disease did. I say that humorously, obviously, but hopefully the exaggeration underscores how dismal our hopes of reconciliation were.

The turning point, as I now see it, came when my dad's health had deteriorated to the point that he was no longer dangerous to my mom. She made the decision to convince him (and allow him) to come back and live with her so that she could care for him in his final days. The process was slow, and I'm not saying everything healed perfectly. However, I can say that our family was able to experience the last several months of my dad's life *together*. It wasn't always pretty, but we were able to be by his side until—and through—the very end. Actually, some of those moments toward the end proved to be the most memorable and beautiful of my life. One in particular I'll never forget.

On that weekend I had preached my sermon at our Saturday night service and then preached it again for our 9:30 a.m. service on Sunday. Normally I would have preached it one last time at 11:30 a.m., but something told me not to stay for the 11:30 service. I instructed the team to play back the video of my sermon for the different locations where our church meets. Then I left in my car.

I didn't know where I was going. At first I headed toward my house, but while I was en route, something told me to go to my parents' home instead, which was only a few miles from my own.

When I got there, my dad was pulling up the 11:30 worship experience online to watch in his bed. He had long since passed the point of being able to come to church, but he never missed a sermon on his iPad, which my mom had rigged to the side of his bed where he could mostly control it.

He was confused when I walked in. "Wait, if you're here . . . Who's preaching?" he asked.

"I am."

"But you're here."

I said, "They're going to play the video. I'm going to watch it with you."

I sat on the bed by my dad and watched myself preach. It was a little awkward but mostly very special. There had been a point during our relational standoff where he gave me an ultimatum in anger.

"If you really cared about me, you would cancel one of your preaching engagements and come spend time with *me*."

I remembered him having said that as I was leaving that day, and as he was giving me a few pointers, but mostly telling me how much he enjoyed watching me preach. I remember that day's conversation pretty vividly, because it would be the last coherent conversation I would ever have with my dad.

That night my mom called me and said, "He doesn't have long. Get over here now."

He died a few days later with his family by his side singing his favorite hymns like "The Old Rugged Cross," "Jesus Keep Me Near the Cross," and "Bad Moon Rising" by Credence Clearwater Revival. Hey, it's kind of a hymn.

I was reading him a sermon by Charles Spurgeon called "The Peculiar Sleep of the Beloved" when he took his last breath. It was a surreal experience, compounded in significance by the complications surrounding it.

I've thought a lot about my dad's death and how my faith helps me to interpret it.

Literally for years, I prayed for God to heal my dad's body. Healing—that's the thing I wanted. That's the thing I thought we needed. That's the thing I couldn't stop wishing for, even as I wondered why it wouldn't happen. You could say I thirsted for it.

And in an eternal sense, I do believe God healed my dad. In heaven he doesn't have ALS or mental disorders. I believe he watches me preach on heaven's own livestream, where there is never any buffering.

But of course that isn't the kind of healing I had in mind while I was praying. So what did God have in mind?

I don't believe God gave my dad a disease or took pleasure in his suffering. But I've begun to think there were some reasons behind why God did not heal my dad in this life. I can't see it all, but I sense there's meaning there, probably many layers and angles of meaning. I know it was healing for years of relational stuff when my mom made the decision to welcome him back and care for him in his dying days. I know I had to get past some of my own pride to be able to reconcile with my dad. Some things that needed to happen, happened because my father wasn't "healed" the way we asked for.

Just like my father in his illness, and just like Jesus dying of dehydration and asphyxiation on the cross, we all have distresses in life, both physical ailments and emotional troubles. Those of us who are on spiritual journeys are not immune to the effects of living in a fallen world. And in fact, we may have additional hardships that others don't because we are targets of persecution and spiritual attack.

What are *your* troubles? What do *you* thirst for?

"I am thirsty for this illness to end."

"I am thirsty for my marriage to get better."

"I am thirsty for a job."

"I am thirsty for respect."

"I am thirsty to do something that matters."

"I am thirsty for my son to get his life together."

"I am thirsty to defeat my addiction."

"I am thirsty to find a boyfriend."

"I am thirsty for the pain to go away."

"I am thirsty for my coworkers to stop making fun of my faith."

Whatever you are thirsting for, there are two things that will help you uncover the meaning in your distress: trust and time. Just as going through a dark night of the soul can be a part of your spiritual maturing, so enduring distress with faith helps to mold you into someone who is more like Christ. Jesus's distress on the cross didn't mean his situation was hopeless, and neither should your distresses cause you to lose hope.

Jesus knew in advance that he would be successful in his mission on the cross. That's why he said beforehand, "In this world you will have trouble. But take heart! I have overcome the world."[1]

Strike the Rock

Our biological need for hydration is so great that when we are thirsty it gets to be like we can't think of anything else. And when our need is that urgent, we can lose all sense of perspective.

Two times the Hebrew people got in trouble over water while they were in the desert of Sinai. Now, in fairness, you can understand why. Sinai is one of the driest places on earth. Parts of it get less than two inches of rain per year. It has little surface water except after the occasional flash flood.

Once, while the Hebrews were wandering in this wilderness under Moses, they came to their leader demanding water.[2] Since it looked like they were going to die of thirst, they questioned whether God was even with them. It was sort of a dark night of the soul that the whole community participated in. They asked, "Is the Lord among us or not?" God miraculously provided water by having Moses strike a rock with his staff. After that, the people quieted down.

Later, though, a similar situation occurred where the people quarreled with Moses.[3] "There is no water to drink!" they lamented. Moses got mad. And this time, it was Moses who got in trouble. Again, he struck the rock and got water out of it, but God accused Moses of not having faith in him. We're not sure what exactly Moses did wrong. Maybe the problem was that Moses struck the rock *twice,* because once should have been enough if he really trusted God. Some have drawn conclusions on the more elaborate implications of the rock as a type of Christ, who was struck once for our sins.

Whatever the hidden meaning of Moses's failure might be, we need to recognize that the New Testament applies these events to Christians. Referring to the ancient Israelites, it says, "They drank from the spiritual rock that accompanied them, and that rock was Christ."[4] The water that the Israelites drank was a form of deliverance for them, and all deliverance ultimately comes from the Savior of the world, Jesus Christ. He is still the miraculous rock of grace and salvation for us today. He is the source that satisfies our thirst.

And this is the point I want you to remember when the distress in your life becomes so great that you find yourself in desperation mode: We have to go to the right source of water for our thirst. We have to go to Jesus for help.

Some of the Israelites in the Sinai desert were faithful to God, their deliverer, and some were not. Let's learn from their example. When we have physical distresses of any kind, whether illness, injury, weakness, or whatever it may be, Christ our spiritual Rock is sufficient to satisfy our needs.

The sooner we learn this lesson, the better. Because our vulnerability to hardship and distress is not going to go away. If anything, we'll get weaker and more vulnerable as we go on in life.

Fragile Jars

If you think you've got a lot of physical distresses to endure on your own journey, compare yourself with the apostle Paul.

For one thing, the apostle Paul had a "thorn" in the flesh that tormented him.[5] Although no one can say definitively, the thorn is believed by many to have been a chronic health condition.

He was also the "poster apostle" for the principle that serving God does not necessarily shelter us from harm but can actually expose us to more of it. He didn't like to brag about what he'd been through, but on one occasion some people dragged his history of hardship and persecution out of him:

I have worked much harder, been in prison more fre-
quently, been flogged more severely, and been exposed
to death again and again. Five times I received from the
Jews the forty lashes minus one. Three times I was beaten
with rods, once I was pelted with stones, three times I was
shipwrecked, I spent a night and a day in the open sea, I
have been constantly on the move. I have been in danger
from rivers, in danger from bandits, in danger from my
fellow Jews, in danger from Gentiles; in danger in the city,
in danger in the country, in danger at sea; and in danger
from false believers. I have labored and toiled and have
often gone without sleep; I have known hunger and thirst
and have often gone without food; I have been cold and
naked. Besides everything else, I face daily the pressure of
my concern for all the churches.[6]

When Paul went through all this, he must have thought often
about the suffering that Jesus endured after being arrested and
when he was on the cross. In fact, we know that Paul saw a conti-
nuity between Jesus's suffering and his own. "I rejoice in what I
am suffering for you," he told one congregation, "and I fill up in
my flesh what is still lacking in regard to Christ's afflictions, for
the sake of his body, which is the church."[7] It's not that Paul
thought Jesus's suffering was inadequate. Instead, Paul apparently
believed that the preaching of the gospel would in a sense extend
Christ's beneficial suffering throughout history.

Paul once referred to our physical bodies as "jars of clay," or vessels that are useful for containing something valuable (the gospel) but that are fragile and will only last for a while.[8] But he went on to say that the power of the Resurrection life of Jesus enabled him to endure adversity. "We always carry around in our body the death of Jesus, so that the life of Jesus may also be revealed in our body. For we who are alive are always being given over to death for Jesus' sake, so that his life may also be revealed in our mortal body."[9]

Whether our physical distresses come directly from service to Christ, or whether they are just a part of living as fallen people in a fallen world, God's strength can shine through them. As God reassured Paul, "My power is made perfect in weakness."[10] This caused Paul not to complain about his weakness, much less to despair about it, but instead to boast in it, because it was in his weakness that Christ's power displayed itself. He said, "For Christ's sake, I delight in weaknesses, in insults, in hardships, in persecutions, in difficulties. For when I am weak, then I am strong."[11]

The child's song we all learned is pretty, but maybe not very accurate. It's not "they are weak but he is strong."[12] The truth is, "I am weak but, because he is strong and because he is in me, then I am strong in my weakness." It doesn't sing quite as well, but it's a much more powerful thought, don't you think?

Are you able to look at your pain, your weakness, your distresses that way? I'm not sure I'm there yet, honestly. But that's what maturity looks like. It's an attitude that develops as we continue in our journey with Jesus. You can learn to find God's grace in the midst of distress.

Your body is a fragile jar—but it holds the imperishable message of the gospel.

You are going to be weak sometimes—and that's when Christ is going to be strongest in you.

Your thirst serves a purpose.

The Woman and the Two Wells

One time during his earthly ministry, Jesus was traveling through Samaria and he got thirsty, just as he later would on the cross. So around noon he stopped beside Jacob's well in the little town of Sychar. Soon along came a woman to draw water. Jesus asked this woman for a drink.[13]

Now, a Jewish rabbi like Jesus was not supposed to associate with a Samaritan woman, but Jesus wasn't afraid to break the religious rules of the day. He did things his way. So he didn't hesitate to talk to this woman.

The woman was surprised, perhaps offended at the request, and scoffed at the idea that Jesus was asking her to give him water.

Jesus could have said, "Woman, I'm not asking you for water simply because I'm thirsty. If I were that thirsty, I would hit this well with a stick and make water come out like Moses did with a rock." But he didn't say that. He was trying to affect change through her, going beyond physical need to spiritual need. So he said, "If you knew the gift of God and who it is that asks you for a drink, you would have asked him and he would have given you living water."[14]

Much like the two people on the road to Emmaus, this woman had no idea whom she was standing next to. She had no idea what he was capable of. And so she said to him, "Sir, . . . you have nothing to draw with and the well is deep. Where can you get this living water?"[15]

Any time when you're talking to Jesus and you start a sentence with the phrase "You have nothing . . ." whatever you say next is wrong. Later, his disciples would think that Jesus had nothing to feed a group of five thousand-plus people, but Jesus would say, "Just bring me a fish and chips combo, do what I say, and everybody goes home . . . with a doggie bag."[16] When you have Jesus, you have everything you need.

Jesus didn't need a bucket to draw water from a well. He himself was the source of the living water he'd been talking about. I heard one preacher explain the irony in how this woman had come to a well, but more importantly, she had met a well.

Jesus proceeded to get the conversation back on track. What this woman had come to get (water from Jacob's well) wasn't what she most needed (living water within herself). And Jesus wanted to deal with her real need. It's not unusual, actually, for God to bypass what you hope for to give you what you really need. Jesus said to the woman, "Everyone who drinks this water will be thirsty again, but whoever drinks the water I give them will never thirst.

Indeed, the water I give them will become in them a spring of water welling up to eternal life."[17]

The woman didn't quite get it yet, though she was getting closer. "Sir," she said, "give me this water so that I won't get thirsty and have to keep coming here to draw water."[18]

Jesus said, "Go, call your husband and come back."[19]

On the surface, this sounds like a nice invitation. You know, "I want to meet Bob." But this woman's situation was—how should I put it? Complicated.

She replied, "I have no husband."[20]

Jesus agreed with her. "You are right when you say you have no husband."

At this point she must have been thinking, *Boy, I dodged a bullet on this one. I came out here at noon so I wouldn't run into anybody who knows my shady history with men. Then I met this stranger. And fortunately he's assuming that I'm simply single. Thank goodness he doesn't know my past.* But her relief was short-lived. Because Jesus, who could read the hearts of all people, went on to tell her that he knew about her five ex-husbands and the guy she was shacking up with at the time. He wasn't trying to embarrass her, much less impress her with his knowledge. He was trying to surface her real need. It's like he was saying to her, "Your issue is that you've been going for 'water' in all the wrong places. You've had five husbands, and now there's this friend with benefits. And you're still not satisfied."

This conversation was getting really personal really fast, and so the woman tried to deflect by bringing up a theological point of difference between Samaritans and Jews. But finally it came down to Jesus's identity, as it always does. Like the two people on the road to Emmaus, this woman got a revelation of who Jesus really was.

She said, "I know that Messiah . . . is coming. When he comes, he will explain everything to us."[21]

Jesus couldn't have been more clear about his messiahship when he said, "I, the one speaking to you—I am he."[22]

The woman at the well is you and she's me—you know that, right? At times we all get "thirsty" for something and look in wrong places to satisfy our need.

God is saying to us, "I'm the one. I'm the well. I'm the one you've been looking for. I'm the one you've been spending your whole life trying to find, but you didn't know where to look. I'm the one!"

Choose Your Well

Many times we find ourselves unsatisfied in life. We get to a place where we wonder if anything means anything. Often it's because we're drinking from the wrong wells. We're drinking from wells and cisterns that, as the Bible says, are cracked.[23]

Let's make it personal. What are the wrong wells that you've tried to drink from in your life?

Maybe one's a relationship. You tried to put somebody else in the place of God and that person let you down, because people always will.

Maybe one's a certain level of accomplishment. You thought once you got it you would be completely set, and then you got it and you still felt unstable.

Jesus Christ is the only true source of satisfaction. That's why Jesus told the woman at the well, "If you drink from this well, you're going to be thirsty again."

When I was a little boy, I remember going to the beach and getting desperately thirsty while swimming. So, of course, I'd drink the saltwater. And, of course, I just got thirstier, and I didn't understand why. Water, water everywhere, and not a drop to drink.[24]

So many things in our lives promise to give us satisfaction but let us down in the end. They're just not capable of giving us all we want and all we need. But Jesus is a well that satisfies. And if we would learn to drink more deeply from this well, our thirst would be quenched.

If you're going to thirst, thirst for the right thing—thirst for God. Like the psalmist who said,

> You, God, are my God,
>   earnestly I seek you;
> I thirst for you,
>   my whole being longs for you,
> in a dry and parched land
>   where there is no water.[25]

'The good news is that the emptiness you feel in human relationships and in things of this world can serve to lead you to a well that will never run dry. They remind you that you need a source that is greater. They can drive you to God.

He invites you freely to come to him for satisfaction. You don't have to earn living water. Jesus paid for it and gives it freely. As Isaiah 55 says,

Come, all you who are thirsty,
     come to the waters;
and you who have no money,
     come, buy and eat![26]

I love how we can come to the waters, even though we're poor and destitute, because Jesus paid the price in full for us to drink freely from the well of his love.

The Purpose in Your Pain

What kept Jesus going through his long, agonizing hours of thirst and other suffering on the cross? It was his knowledge of the purpose in the pain. He was accomplishing something. He had a reason for what he was doing, and as awful as the suffering was, it was worth it.

There is a purpose in *your* pain too. A way that the living water will flow through you.

God is accomplishing something through the struggles you face today. He is accomplishing something when your health falters. He is accomplishing something when your heart is broken. He is accomplishing something when a dream comes to an end.

Although your struggle with the hard things in life will never be finished until you see Jesus face to face, there's a sense in which you can know today that God will perfect that which concerns you.

I hesitate to say some of these things because it might feel like I'm attempting to minimize, overspiritualize, or make light of your suffering. That is not my intention. I just want to comfort you by reminding you that your pain doesn't have to be meaningless. When you remember there is a reason for the cross, it is easier to bear.

When you exercise your body, it hurts because the muscle fibers are tearing apart. But you push through the pain because you know it's achieving a purpose. There's a purpose to the pain.

There's also pain when you're injured, such as when a bone is broken or a ligament is torn. But you don't push through that pain, because there would be no purpose to it. You'd only make things worse.

In your suffering, what you need is to know what Jesus knew—that there is a purpose to your pain. There is sanctification in your suffering. You can push through it until it's passed.

What purpose might God be working out through your

pain? Ask him to reveal it to you. And ask him to help you live into the purpose. Although it may not change your outer circumstances, it will transform your inner life. It will conform you more and more to the image of Christ.

Digging a Well

When the soldier pierced Jesus's side and water and blood flowed out, it was so that our thirst could be satisfied. When God had his Son die on a cross and dug a grave to bury his body, he was digging a well. Jesus would rise up in resurrection power just as the living water of his Spirit springs up within us. He is a source of satisfaction that can never be depleted.

And when you have to go through hard things in life, God is digging a well within you. When you are disappointed or hurt, God is digging a well within. When things happen that you don't understand, he's digging a well. When people you care about walk away, God is digging a well. He's digging a well, and living water will flow from it.

As the miles pass in the journey of our lives, even with Jesus by our side, we will have times of deep distress. But the words "I am thirsty" remind us of a well that never runs dry. There is a source of satisfaction that can never run out.

Our journey's destination is heaven, where we will enjoy the sight and the presence of God forever. We'll talk more about that in Mile 7. But for now, here's a foretaste:

Never again will they hunger;

    never again will they thirst.

The sun will not beat down on them,

    nor any scorching heat.

For the Lamb at the center of the throne will be

        their shepherd;

    he will lead them to springs of living water.[27]

A WORD OF
TRIUMPH

"It is finished."

—John 19:30

There was never a case of snatching victory out of the jaws of defeat like what Jesus accomplished at Calvary. His enemies milling around the cross must have thought they had him beat. His greatest enemy, the devil, must have looked on at the scene of crucifixion with glee. *But even as his opponents scribbled an L in Jesus's column, heaven was etching a permanent W.* The Resurrection was still to come, of course, but it was now a foregone conclusion.

Be sure to see how spacious Jesus's win was. Like David going up against Goliath in a mano-a-mano battle, Jesus our champion scored a victory for his whole side, including you and me. All the setbacks we experience in our journey through life, all the hardships we have to endure, all our own failures—they're all redeemed in the Great Reversal of Jesus's victory.

Jesus went straight from a pitiful last word of distress—"I am thirsty"—to a heroic last word of triumph: "When he had received the drink, Jesus said, 'It is finished.'"[1]

It's interesting that this "word" is so vague, isn't it? "It is finished" has a subtle subversive quality. It reveals how Jesus sabotaged the plans of the devil as well as those of his human enemies. It simply represents the greatest, most incredible turnaround in the history of humankind.

Jesus had already had this in mind at the Last Supper when he prayed to the Father, "I have brought you glory on earth by finishing the work you gave me to do."[2] Now this *claim* was fully and absolutely true.

In the Greek language in which the gospel of John was written, "It is finished" is one word: *Tetelestai*. "Done!"

That same word appears just two verses earlier. We saw it when we learned about the fifth "word" from the cross. *"Knowing that everything had now been finished,* and so that Scripture would be fulfilled, Jesus said, 'I am thirsty.'"[3] Everything had now been finished.

Tetelestai. Done. Over.

But before we get too caught up in celebrating the victory, we should ask ourselves, what exactly was it that was finished?

Obviously, Jesus's ordeal on the cross was finished. He had drunk the bitter cup of his sufferings to its dregs, and now the cup was drained. Very shortly afterward, he would bow his head and give up his spirit.[4]

But his suffering was not all that was finished . . .

- Jesus's whole life's work was finished. From his birth as a baby in a stable, to hiding out in a foreign land during his toddler years, to the obedience of growing up as a human son, to the humbling of his baptism and the hardship of his temptation, to the preaching to the crowds, to the press of people wanting his miracles, to nights spent in prayer, to his disappointments in the men he was trying to make his representatives, to the opposition from religious leaders, to the spiritual agony in Gethsemane, to his arrest and the whole bloody mess that followed—it was all done, all over with, all complete now.

- As a result, Jesus's mission to win redemption for sinners was finished. The Passover Lamb had been slain, and its sweet savor was rising to heaven. He had completed the sacrifice necessary to atone for the sins of the world.

- Furthermore, the Old Testament prophecies of the Messiah's earthly coming were finished. That's what Jesus disclosed to the two disciples on the road to Emmaus. As hard as it could be for people to get their minds around it, Jesus had fulfilled the predictions perfectly.

- The Old Testament Law was finished in the sense that its inner meaning was fulfilled in the grace that Jesus established for us at the cross.

- The priesthood and its sacrifices, along with the whole system of symbolism represented in temple-based worship, was finished. This too was fulfilled in Jesus's dual role as High Priest and Sacrifice at the cross.

- The mastery of the devil was finished. As the first prophecy in the Bible says, Eve's offspring (Jesus), having been bruised in the heel by the serpent (his murder on the cross inspired by the devil), had crushed the serpent's head (robbed the devil's power).[5]

- Your hopelessness and mine about our ability to
  triumph over our own shortcomings and the stresses
  of a temporary earthly life were finished too. We
  share in the victory through faith.

The sixth "word" isn't the last one. But it's the climax of the great drama of Calvary.

When we're feeling defeated, what we need to remember is that *all is well* in the end because of Jesus's triumph in ending the power of sin, death, and the devil over us.

QUESTIONS FOR YOU

- *What are the areas of your life where you long for victory today?*
- *What has been causing you to lose or to fail in those areas?*
- *What might a win look like there?*
- *Are you ready to trust God to bring about a good outcome in his way and in his time? Why?*
- *What sustains your faith in God's willingness and ability to give you victory?*
- *How often do you think about your eventual death? When you do think about death, how much fear does it inspire in you?*
- *How does the promise of resurrection inspire you?*

Out of the Jaws
of Defeat

I've observed that a lot of people, when they watch a film about the crucifixion of Christ or they read about Jesus dying, start to cry. It's almost as if they feel sorry for Jesus. As if they pity him.

I believe Jesus would say the same thing to them that he said to Mary Magdalene in the garden on Resurrection day: "Why are you crying?"[1] And he would add, "Don't feel sorry for me. I'm not dead. I'm alive!"

And so when we come to the Son of God, we don't come to someone who is to be pitied in his death but to someone who established his own might in his death. Jesus was once a Suffering Servant, but he is one no longer. He's the risen King of kings and he reigns in power.

His sixth "word" from the cross is a shout of victory. He won, and all with him win too.

As I've said in the last couple of chapters, there's no doubt that those of us who are on a spiritual journey with Jesus are subject to dangers and trials in this world. We even have some additional spiritual risks and vulnerabilities to persecution that those who are not following Jesus don't have to deal with. But none of this means defeat.

Think about the seeming defeats in your life right now. Those areas where it looks like you're going to fall short.

Maybe you've been struggling to get over some kind of sin habit or addiction, and you haven't gotten anywhere.

Maybe you've been trying to restore a relationship, but so far the doors remain shut.

Maybe you did what everybody says you should do—you went after a big dream—and it ended in humiliating failure.

Maybe you've fought a battle against injustice or unfairness, and the other side has prevailed.

Maybe you've received a medical diagnosis, and you're facing the fact that you'll never regain full health.

Discouraging, to be sure. But is this really the end of hope for you?

I can't promise that you will have exactly the kind of victory you want in this life (though it may be more possible than you think!). But I can definitely tell you that, if you are traveling through this life with Jesus, then in one way or another, at one time or another, all your defeats will be overwhelmed in Christ's victory.

As we saw in the last chapter, the apostle Paul suffered more than most people do. Yet he showed the resilience of the true follower of Jesus. He said, "We are hard pressed on every side, but not crushed; perplexed, but not in despair; persecuted, but not abandoned; struck down, but not destroyed."[2] That's our reality too.

Ultimately, the message of the cross to us is not a message of defeat but of triumph. We may lose some battles along the way, but the war is going to end in our favor. We participate in the victory Jesus has already secured.

The Finishing Touches

Picture this. Someone has become sick and has been admitted to a hospital and yet has continued getting worse. The doctors have been trying to keep this person alive with procedures and medicine. Now the family members of the sick person are in the hospital waiting room nervously wondering whether their loved one is going to live or die.

A doctor comes out with a serious face and says to the family, "I'm sorry. There's nothing more we can do." It's obvious to the family members what that means. There are no more treatment options. The case is hopeless. The sick person is going to die.

When Jesus said, "It is finished," the enemies of the gospel must have heard him making this kind of announcement: "There's nothing more I can do. It's over." But really what Jesus was saying was "There's nothing more I need to do. I've accomplished my mission. I've won."

Even today, people get his meaning mixed up all the time— they don't understand what he did on the cross. It's not just unbelievers and the irreligious who make this mistake. Those of us who are on a spiritual journey with Jesus can get mixed up about him too. The reality of grace is just so hard to get our minds around.

See, many people spell the essence of Christianity this way: D-O. "Do this, this, and this to be saved." But that was the message of the law that we could never keep. The law says we're supposed to do or not do things. It's all about restriction.

The gospel is a message of resurrection, not restriction. You and I aren't saved because of what we do or don't do. We are saved because of what was done. The gospel's other name is spelled D-O-N-E.

This is true, not just when we come to Jesus for salvation in the first place, but also when we are trying to be rescued from the power of sin daily. We're totally forgiven, and it's Jesus's power that makes it possible for us to convert our official position with God into actual, everyday victory over sin.

I see a lot of people trying to put the finishing touches on their lives so God will accept them. They think that if they clear up this sin area, or if they do that religious activity, God will like them more. There's nothing wrong with a full commitment to obedience to God. But if we think we need to do these kinds of things so that we will have a full relationship with God, we've got it all wrong.

Jesus has already put the finishing touches on our salvation. He has already delivered the deathblow to darkness. It changes everything if we understand the true meaning of triumph.

So if we are not supposed to try to add to Jesus's work, what *are* we supposed to do?

Our response to Christ should be, "I know that if I lived a thousand lifetimes I could never fulfill the righteous requirements of the law. And I don't need to anyway. You've already done everything that was needed. So I give you my life today, tomorrow, and every day."

An old hymn says, "Jesus paid it all," and then goes on to say, "All to him I owe."[3] That doesn't mean that when we pay him by trying to do good, our salvation will be complete. It means that in responding to what has already been paid, we owe him our lives.

What freedom would it bring you if you understood today, at a new level, that Christian faith isn't about a bad person becoming better but instead is about a dead person being made alive?[4]

What would it mean for you today to look at the guilt and the condemnation, the power that sin held over you, and realize it's all gone?

How would your relationship with God be different if you realized that there was no longer enmity between you and God?

They say that unless you're a trained lifeguard, if you see someone who is in distress in a swimming pool or lake, you're better off not trying to save this person while he or she is thrashing in the water. They say you should wait until the swimmer has settled down or grown weaker. *Then* swim up and begin to haul the person to safety. As long as a person is trying to save himself or herself, you'll only endanger yourself attempting to help that person.

"Cease striving and know that I am God," one psalm says.[5] Cease struggling. Cease thrashing. The salvation of God begins when our human striving ends. Let yourself grow calm and embrace the full acceptance of Jesus Christ, knowing that it has already been secured for you.

You don't have to put the finishing touches on your salvation. Jesus has already done it. You win, because he overcame.

Wreathed in Victory

In ancient Greece, winners of athletic competitions would receive a wreath of fragrant evergreen laurel leaves to wear on their heads. In ancient Rome, military commanders who had been victorious in battle would wear the same kind of wreath to show off. The Caesars, too, would wear laurel wreaths on special occasions and would have their images impressed on coins with their wreaths on display. These wreaths were the crowns of the day, even if they did look like something you could buy on Etsy.

Before crucifying Jesus, the soldiers put a crown of thorns on his head, mocking what they thought were his ridiculous pretensions to being a king.[6] But as we know, he *was* king.

Likewise, Pontius Pilate had a sign attached to Jesus's cross indicating that he was the King of the Jews. The Jewish leaders asked him to change the sign to state, "He claimed to be the King of the Jews," but Pilate refused to make the change.[7] So the sign told the truth. Jesus was the king. He wears an eternal crown today.

The New Testament promises us a crown too if we persevere. If you discipline your behavior like an athlete in training, you will receive a crown that never fades.[8] If you serve God faithfully and with integrity, you will wear a crown of glory.[9] If you endure trials and persecution with faith, you will inherit a crown of life.[10]

Here's what Paul said shortly before his head was lopped off in a Roman prison:

> I am already being poured out like a drink offering, and
> the time for my departure is near. I have fought the good
> fight, I have finished the race, I have kept the faith. Now
> there is in store for me the crown of righteousness, which
> the Lord, the righteous Judge, will award to me on that
> day—and not only to me, but also to all who have longed
> for his appearing.[11]

These lines not only give us encouragement about the victory to come but also teach us how to act in the meantime. If we're engaged in a fight worth fighting, we keep swinging. If we're in a race to a finish line worth getting to, we keep running. We don't give up on the faith, as so many others have done, but we hold on to the truth of the gospel to the end, finishing our journey toward God.

When I was sixteen years old, God called me to start a church. Since then, there have been many times I have been tempted to quit. Keeping up with the pace of growth is a challenge in itself. We've been misunderstood and we've taken criticism, some of it constructive but much of it misplaced and unfair. I get tired. Another Sunday is coming up? Somebody else is looking to me for leadership? Can I continue giving so much of myself year after year? As grateful as I am for my calling, there are times I wonder whether I can make it for the long haul.

Jesus had plenty of reasons to quit in the middle of his ministry. Disciples who were incorrigibly dense and selfish. Crowds who wanted his miracles instead of Jesus himself. Hypocritical religious leaders who kept probing and plotting until they finally took him down.

I think we all know what it is like to want to give up. We all know what it is like for circumstances to turn against us, so that it looks like there's nothing more we can do. We're defeated. But the Spirit of Christ won't allow us to quit. He won't allow us to say "It is finished" until our calling is completed.

This is what Paul specially identifies as a "trustworthy saying":

If we died with him,
    we will also live with him;
if we endure,
    we will also reign with him.[12]

Temporary or apparent defeat may have twisted a painful crown of thorns on your head. But by the grace of God and through the power of faith, it will become an evergreen crown of victory.

Taking Possession

Back in Mile 2, I told you about how at Elevation Church we encourage people to make their commitment to Jesus, receive salvation, and be baptized. "Repent and be baptized" is the normal pattern, dating back to Acts 2:38.

Yet in 2014, Elevation Church started getting criticism for

supposedly manipulating people into going forward for baptism. A local investigative reporter accused us of planting people in the audience who were pretending to be baptized. For the record, the concept of planting people in our church to pretend to be baptized is nauseating to me. Although I believe in grace, I am much too scared of the Old Testament wrath of God to resort to those types of antics. In actuality, we had instructed some volunteers to get up in order to lead the people who made decisions to the places where we were going to baptize them when I made the altar call. We also instructed some of the people who had signed up to be baptized in the months leading up to this event, which was more spontaneous in nature, to go first. But because of what I believe to be irresponsible (and downright despicable) journalism, rumors began to circulate implying that thousands of people who had been baptized in our church were not making a genuine profession of faith.

Now, if you want to pick on me for my haircut, my fashion sense or lack thereof, the house I live in, my Instagram posts, or even the way I preach, okay. Go for it. But it's different territory when you attack people who have been baptized into the family of God at our church. These were sincere faith decisions by precious people who had one of the most meaningful experiences of their lives.

I don't mind telling you, I felt a sense of righteous indignation (a spiritual way to say, I was fighting mad!) about the allegations. But how was I going to respond?

A friend called me who has been in ministry longer than I have been alive. He had seen the news reports and was as mad as

I was. He used some pretty un-preacherly words. Then he asked what I had been wondering, "What are you going to do about it?"

I said, "I don't know. I don't want to be defensive." I didn't want to go to the pulpit the next Sunday and turn my preaching into an occasion for a news conference. That's not what the pulpit is for, in my view.

When I hung up the phone with him, I felt like God said to me, *"If you don't want to be defensive, then don't play defense. Go on the offensive."*

So that's what we did. The following weekend, I announced what our response would be: we'd be holding *another* baptism that Sunday night! And that night was one of our most remarkable worship services ever, as hundreds more people were baptized as a declaration of their faith in Jesus Christ. What seemed like an attack actually served to advance the gospel.

God is in the victory business . . . when his people commit to playing offense rather than declaring defeat.

Put to Good Use

In my book *Sun Stand Still,* I dared readers to have audacious faith and ask God for the impossible. I don't think you can actually read your Bible and come to any other conclusion: God works miracles to give his people victories that are impossible by human standards.

One old man named Moses with a staff extracting an entire slave population from Egypt?

A farmer named Gideon defeating the Midianite army with a mere three hundred men?

A teenage boy named David defeating a giant in battle?

A fisherman named Peter becoming the "rock" on which Jesus built his church?

So if you're looking up at a wall that seems way too high for you to scale, don't give in to defeat. Ask God to help you get over the wall . . . or knock it down! Why wouldn't you? He "is able to do immeasurably more than all we ask or imagine, according to his power that is at work within us."[13]

But what if he says no? *No, I won't give her to you as your wife. No, I won't take away the multiple sclerosis. No, I won't prevent your business from going belly-up. I, who felt the pain of letting my Son die on the cross, understand your suffering better than anyone. I'm with you at all times to comfort you. Still, the answer to your request is no.* What then?

Even when our victories don't come in this life, we are still victors.

We have this promise: "In all things God works for the good of those who love him, who have been called according to his purpose."[14] That doesn't mean we won't have bad things happen in life. It does mean God converts those bad things to good uses. Sin, opposition, scarcity, failure, even death—it all gets swept up in God's grand plan for Jesus to "reconcile to himself all things, whether things on earth or things in heaven, by making peace through his blood, shed on the cross."[15]

As I quoted earlier, Jesus said, "I have overcome the world!"[16] Because of his victory, we too are overcomers, according to Scripture. "Everyone born of God overcomes the world. This is the victory that has overcome the world, even our faith. Who is it that overcomes the world? Only the one who believes that Jesus is the Son of God."[17]

Our victory comes in walking with Jesus through life, becoming like him and seeking to know him ever better. We are conquerors and "more than conquerors"—that's like saying we are super conquerors. Not because we are super men and women but because we follow a supernatural Victor.

Let me quote Paul on this point at length because it is so powerful:

> If God is for us, who can be against us? He who did not spare his own Son, but gave him up for us all—how will he not also, along with him, graciously give us all things? Who will bring any charge against those whom God has chosen? It is God who justifies. Who then is the one who condemns? No one. Christ Jesus who died—more than that, who was raised to life—is at the right hand of God and is also interceding for us. Who shall separate us from the love of Christ? Shall trouble or hardship or persecution or famine or nakedness or danger or sword?
>
> No, in all these things we are more than conquerors through him who loved us. For I am convinced that

neither death nor life, neither angels nor demons, neither the present nor the future, nor any powers, neither height nor depth, nor anything else in all creation, will be able to separate us from the love of God that is in Christ Jesus our Lord.[18]

The Last Enemy

There's one kind of defeat that we all must face eventually. It's one most of us don't like to talk about or even think about if we can help it. When we do honestly face it, it can plunge us into anguish like Jesus felt at Gethsemane.

Death.

Here is the final seeming defeat that we must endure in our mortal lives. Its gaping mouth awaits and will swallow each one of us sooner or later. As the Bible says, it's the "last enemy."[19]

Except it's an enemy that Jesus has already faced and triumphed over on our behalf. Not that we don't still have to go through the eventual failure of our bodies. But what we must face is only a physical death and not a spiritual one. After the death of our bodies, our spirits keep on going without a moment's interruption, just as Jesus's did when he died on the cross. On to paradise.

If death were truly final, we would have a six-mile miracle at best. But I assure you there is another mile still to come. And so death doesn't warrant all the fear we give to it.

We have Jesus to thank for that. "Since the children have flesh and blood, he too shared in their humanity so that by his death he might break the power of him who holds the power of death—that is, the devil—and free those who all their lives were held in slavery by their fear of death."[20]

Even this final and greatest of the defeats we endure in life will be reversed. Death seemed to have Jesus in its giant jaws of defeat. But Jesus opened his mouth to say, "It is finished," and the devourer was devoured. "Death has been swallowed up in victory."[21]

When Jesus hung on the cross, his detractors mocked him for supposedly not being able to save himself from death. I love how the Bible turns around and mocks death because of Jesus's resurrection. This is premium trash talk from the ultimate victor. Paul said, "Where, O death, is your victory? Where, O death, is your sting?"[22]

If it weren't for Jesus, death would still have its sting. If we really did have to put the finishing touches on our triumph, death would still have the victory over us. "But thanks be to God!" Paul exclaimed. "He gives us the victory through our Lord Jesus Christ."[23]

What does this mean for us now? Paul tells us. "Therefore, my dear brothers and sisters, stand firm. Let nothing move you."[24] Christ's victory fills us with confidence to deal with what we're facing now.

If you're misunderstood, stand firm.

If you're tempted, stand firm.

If you're hurting, stand firm.

If you're fearful, stand firm.

If you're in trouble, stand firm.

Keep your faith. Be constant in doing what you know you ought to do. Hold on to your hope. Look ahead in expectancy. Even be lighthearted, because you know that defeat is only for a while, whereas victory is forever.

Triumph lies just ahead.

Finished and Done

Jesus's sixth "word" from the cross was so loud that it echoes to the end of history. Don't believe me?

The apostle John—the only apostle who was there as a witness of Jesus's sayings on the cross—later in his life received a vision of the nature of history's conclusion. He saw the new heavens and the new earth. He saw a new Jerusalem descend from heaven. He saw Jesus sit on the throne and ask John to take some notes for him.

And what was the very thing Jesus asked John to record? We read it in Revelation 21: "It is done."[25]

It is done! It is finished!

Jesus called himself "the Alpha and the Omega, the Beginning and the End." He is the starting line and the finish line of our journey. In history, in our lives right now, he is establishing victory through the authority he confirmed by his death and resurrection.

I feel defeated sometimes when our church and I, as its pastor, face opposition and setbacks. I feel defeated sometimes when I have a problem in a relationship that matters to me. I *hate* death, which has taken away my dad and others I love.

But I've seen again and again how God has brought good out of these defeating realities. He's surprised me in ways that I could never have imagined. And I believe that even when I come to the end of my days I'll be able to close my eyes in death and open them in eternal light.

Look at the very next lines of Revelation 21, because they're like a piece of the map showing us what the last three miles of our journey look like:[26]

- "To the thirsty I will give water without cost from the spring of the water of life." (The fifth mile.)
- "Those who are victorious will inherit all this." (The sixth mile.)
- "And I will be their God and they will be my children." (The seventh mile.)

It's all coming together, see?

And union with God, our destination, is what we will look at next.

A WORD OF
REUNION

"Father, into your hands
I commit my spirit."

—Luke 23:46

cripture says, "Jesus knew . . . that he had come from God and was returning to God."[1] After six hours on the cross, the time came for him to be reunited with the Father. That's what was intended for him all along. He was also going ahead to prepare a place for all those who believe in him, so that we can be united with God too.[2]

Usually, people who were crucified died silently, having become so exhausted that they lost the ability to raise themselves up and take a breath, much less speak.

Jesus was not usual. He spoke loudly and boldly at the end. He wanted everybody to know what was going on.

First, he exclaimed out loud in an agony of spirit, "My God, my God, why have you forsaken me?"

Then, after saying to those at the foot of his cross, "I am thirsty," and receiving a drink, he declared victoriously, "It is finished."

Finally, "Jesus called out with a loud voice, 'Father, into your hands I commit my spirit.' When he had said this, he breathed his last."[3]

Jesus—a man who knew, loved, and personally fulfilled the Hebrew Scriptures—died with a verse from the Bible on his lips. In committing his spirit into the hands of God, he was quoting Psalm 31:5. And these words show us a couple of important things about this unusual death.

The first thing we learn is that Jesus's life was not taken from him. He gave it up voluntarily. His spirit wasn't being ripped from his body by forces out of his control; he was intentionally turning it over to God.

Earlier, Jesus had told his disciples that he had the right and the power to choose his death and resurrection. "The reason my Father loves me," he said, "is that I lay down my life—only to take it up again. No one takes it from me, but I lay it down of my own accord. I have authority to lay it down and authority to take it up again."[4] He was no passive victim, as he appeared to onlookers, but instead he was the active agent in his sacrificial death.

The second thing we learn about Jesus's death from his seventh and last "word" on the cross is that he trusted the Father. Despite the temporary sense of abandonment he felt during the hours of darkness, he knew his Father loved him and would receive his spirit upon his death. Jesus remained faithful to the very end.

Philippians 2 shows us *the nature of Jesus's union with* the Father.[5]

Before coming to earth, Jesus was "in very nature God," enjoying the splendors of heaven in the company of the Father and the Holy Spirit. What was their union and delight in one another like? Our closest, purest relationships can only give us a hint of it.

Yet Jesus "did not consider equality with God something to be used to his own advantage." Instead, he chose to use his divinity for our advantage. He "made himself nothing by taking the very nature of a servant, being made in human likeness."

During his earthly life, he was anointed by the Holy Spirit, and he kept in intimate contact with the Father through prayer. But still, it must not have been the same kind of closeness with the other members of the Trinity that he had experienced before.

He did all that the Father asked of him during his thirty-plus years on earth. And finally, "he humbled himself" even more than he already had "by becoming obedient to death— even death on a cross!"

What an amazing reunion Jesus *experienced—and enabled for us—*when at last he went back to the Father!

QUESTIONS FOR YOU

- *When have you felt the closest to God?*
- *What experiences or practices help to draw you closer to God?*
- *To you, what does union with God mean? What does it not mean?*
- *What questions do you have about what your existence will be like after you die?*
- *What is your understanding of what it will be like to live in union with God eternally?*

Into the Presence
of God

Many people's refrigerators, I'm sure, look a lot like ours—covered with Christmas cards and grocery lists. But one time I went to a guy's house and noticed that while his fridge was likewise covered, there weren't any pictures of *people* on his refrigerator. No photos of his wife or children. There weren't even any subpar drawings from his kids that he lied and told them were awesome, as all good dads do. Instead, all he had on his refrigerator were postcards of exotic, beautiful places around the world.

"Man, those are some cool postcards on your fridge," I said. "Are those all the places you've been with your family?"

He said, "No, those are all the places I want to go one day. I keep my focus on where I'm going, not on where I've been."

Everyone has the right to choose their own fridge décor. But personally, I think it's best to allow room for both. It's good to reflect on and appreciate where you've been—*and* anticipate where you're headed. The two go hand in hand as you seek to live by faith in the only moment you and I ever truly have—now.

In your journey and mine, we're headed to the most incredible destination imaginable: heaven. As we learned back at Mile 2, heaven is equated with paradise. You can read Revelation 21:1–22:5 if you want to get an idea of what the picture on a postcard from heaven might look like.

When Jesus said, "Father, into your hands I commit my spirit" and breathed his last, his words signified reunion with the Father. His body went into the grave for three days, and in the few weeks that followed he made a post-Resurrection tour, including his seven-mile victory lap with two followers on the Emmaus road. Soon, he would ascend to heaven, and his reunion with the Father and the Holy Spirit would be complete. Because of Jesus, this same complete union with God awaits us at the end of this life.

In a vision of heaven in Revelation, Jesus cries out from his throne, "Look! God's dwelling place is now among the people, and he will dwell with them. They will be his people, and God himself will be with them and be their God."[1] So let's remember that it really isn't heaven itself—the place or dimension—that matters. *It's who's there.* Our ultimate destination isn't a place but a Person. And that Person is already at work within us—at this very moment—as we yield to his Spirit.

Now and Then

Mile 7 foreshadows our experience of union with God after our death. But I want to point out that being in the presence of God in heaven will only be an intensified experience of something we're already experiencing. After all, if we've passed through Miles 1, 2, and 3—if we have been forgiven, received salvation, and been adopted into God's family—then we're already connected to God. In that regard, heaven is the same, only more so.

Consider how we tend to think about eternal life. The way many people talk about it, you would think that eternal life is something they hope to experience for the first time after death. But actually, for Christ followers, it's something we already have. In fact, you could say that eternal life is another way of referring to our whole spiritual journey.

At the Last Supper, Jesus prayed, "Now this is eternal life: that they know you, the only true God, and Jesus Christ, whom you have sent."[2] Eternal life is not just an endless *quantity* of life but also a heightened *quality* of life that comes in relationship with God through Jesus. It's ours as soon as we set out on the seven-mile journey of following Jesus.

Still, eternal life does have a future dimension to it. The New Testament says that eternal life is something we will "reap" eventually.[3] It's something we will "take hold of" after we "fight the good fight of the faith," or complete our journey, as we learned in Mile 6.[4] Our fullest and most direct experience of eternal life is still ahead of us. This gives us hope beyond the brokenness of our earthly experience.

One way to think about the difference between how we live in the presence of God now and how we will live in the presence

of God after death is by thinking of it as having our eyes opened—
fully. Just as the two disciples on the road to Emmaus saw Jesus
but didn't *really* see him until the end of their journey, so we will
eventually have our eyes opened to see God as he truly is. As the
apostle Paul said, "Now we see only a reflection as in a mirror;
then we shall see face to face. Now I know in part; then I shall
know fully, even as I am fully known."[5]

Right now, we walk the miles of our journey "by faith, not by
sight."[6] Jesus told one of the disciples who saw him in his resurrected form, "Because you have seen me, you have believed;
blessed are those who have not seen and yet have believed."[7] That's
us—people who are blessed because, though we haven't seen Jesus
in the flesh, nevertheless we believe in him.

But one day, we won't need our faith to connect us with Jesus.
We'll actually be in his presence. We'll meet him face to face,
walking the rest of the way by sight, not by faith.

A Morsel of Heaven

We began our journey with the story about Jesus traveling with
the two people on the way to Emmaus. And as we approach the
climax of the story on this seventh mile, we are prepared to see our
own part in it.[8]

Remember, Jesus, Cleopas, and Unnamed Follower #2 walked
seven miles to the little town of Emmaus. When they got there,
they apparently came to the two followers' house. There, the two

people invited Jesus to spend the night with them before resuming his journey in the morning. Their hearts had been burning within them while they talked. They wanted the conversation with this extraordinary stranger to go on. So even though Jesus at first politely declined their offer, they pressed him to stay. It was his plan to stay with them all along, but his presence rewards pursuit. And so when they urged him, he agreed.

The three of them sat down to eat. Nothing abnormal about this, right? They had walked for two hours and were hungry. Yet this meant that the right psychological, not to mention theological, moment had arrived. "When he was at the table with them, he took bread, gave thanks, broke it and began to give it to them. Then their eyes were opened and they recognized him."[9]

Isn't that interesting? They hadn't recognized him when he had been preaching to them, but they finally knew who he was when he performed the common, everyday act of breaking bread to distribute it.

What happened? What caused the sudden revelation?

Once, as I was actually visiting the village of Emmaus, our guide offered an explanation that resonated with me. He demonstrated physically how Jesus would have distributed the bread according to Jewish custom. And he showed how, when Jesus offered the bread with palms upturned, the nail scars in his hands would have been exposed. When the followers saw the marks of his suffering, they recognized him for who he really was.

Regardless of the impetus, imagine the shock of this revelation.

The formerly dead Jesus was sitting right here with them, presiding over dinner! They must have had a million questions to ask in that moment.

But before they could ask Jesus the first one, immediately "he disappeared from their sight."[10]

One shock right after another. And how ironic this second one was. The moment the two finally "saw" him, they didn't see him anymore.

They were left to figure out with each other the significance of what they had experienced. What would be the implications of having been reunited with the risen Jesus? Where would the journey of faith lead them now? Perhaps part of the answer to that is symbolized by the very act they were involved in when they realized who they were eating with.

When Jesus broke bread with the two people in Emmaus, he wasn't celebrating the Passover supper. This was just a regular meal. But I have no doubt that, as we read about it, we are supposed to be reminded of how Jesus broke bread just days before with his disciples in the upper room, giving the Passover celebration new meaning by relating it to his upcoming death, and the new future his resurrection would create.

At the Last Supper, Jesus said to his disciples, "I have eagerly desired to eat this Passover with you before I suffer. For I tell you, I will not eat it again until it finds fulfillment in the kingdom of God."[11]

At the Last Supper, Jesus was looking ahead to something

called *the marriage supper of the Lamb*.[12] See, the first Communion celebration in the upper room, along with the millions of Communions that have taken place over the last two thousand years and counting, will culminate in a great gathering in heaven where all of Jesus's followers will celebrate being united with the Lamb who died and rose for them.

It's no mistake that the Bible uses marriage as a persistent symbol for the union of God and his followers. To take just one example, Paul said, "Christ loved the church and gave himself up for her to make her holy, cleansing her by the washing with water through the word, and to present her to himself as a radiant church, without stain or wrinkle or any other blemish, but holy and blameless."[13] Our unity with Jesus is both pure and intimate.

The practice of Communion gives us a hint of it. In taking the bread and cup, we not only look back toward his death but also look forward to the time when we will see Jesus for who he is and will be united with him forever.

And there's still more we can learn from the breaking of bread about how we can live our lives right now.

Taken, Blessed, Broken, Given

I will never forget how my own eyes were opened when my friend, Bishop T.D. Jakes, preached on this very subject. He called attention to the order of Jesus's specific actions when he shared bread with his two followers in Emmaus.[14] He . . .

1. "Took bread"
2. "Gave thanks"
3. "Broke it"
4. "Began to give it to them"

This wasn't the first time Jesus carried out these actions. He took exactly the same four steps, in the same order, when he fed five thousand men, plus women and children, on a slope beside the Sea of Galilee.[15] And again he did the same things at the Last Supper.[16]

Not only is this the pattern of how Jesus served food; it is also the pattern of God's work in our lives. And as Bishop Jakes eloquently illustrated, it is definitely a pattern we see in Scripture.

- *Abraham.* God took Abraham out of Ur of the Chaldeans. He blessed him with Isaac, the son he had prayed for. He broke Abraham on Mount Moriah when he called him to offer up Isaac as a sacrifice. Then he gave Abraham to be the father of many nations.

- *Joseph.* God took Joseph out of the pit where his brothers had left him. He blessed him in the service of Potiphar as the man in charge of the household. He broke him by leaving him in prison for a period. Then he gave him to be the prince of Egypt who would occupy a position where he could save the lives of his people.

- *Moses.* God took Moses, as a baby, from his basket stuck in the river weeds. (In fact, his name means "taken" or "drawn out of.")[17] He blessed him by allowing him to be raised in the house of Pharaoh. He broke Moses during the long years in the wilderness. Yet he also gave him to be the founding leader of his nation.

- *Jesus.* The Son of God was taken from the womb of a virgin named Mary. He was blessed with the ability to teach the truth, perform miracles, and purify the religious system of the day with his grace. He was broken on Mount Calvary for the sins of the world.

And now he has been given as the Savior of the world.

In your life today, you're in one of the stages I just described—taking, blessing, breaking, or giving. In fact, you will find yourself going through all of these stages far more than once, and sometimes, you'll feel like you're in several different stages at the same time.

When you're in the taking stage, it can be uncomfortable. God is taking you out of your comfort zone. He may be taking you out of your job. He may be taking you out of a relationship. He may be taking you out of the place you've lived all your life.

The thing about God taking you is that, while you know what he is taking you from, you may not know where he is taking you to. *What am I supposed to do with myself next?* you ask yourself. The answer isn't clear. All you know is that God is taking you somewhere, and you have to trust that he knows best.

The good news is that God does not "take" in order to deprive you of something. He takes you so that he can bless you. When God is blessing you, it makes all the taking worthwhile.

I know you've had at least a season of your life where God was showing up for you, working through you, and providing for you in ways you could perceive. It's a wonderful place to be.

But after the blessing comes the breaking. And while we all prefer the blessing to the breaking, it was only after the breaking of the bread that the Emmaus followers recognized Jesus for who he was. And it takes breaking for us to recognize him, too.

Maybe your pride has to be broken. Maybe your will has to be broken. Maybe your stubbornness has to be broken. Maybe your self-reliance has to be broken. Maybe some of your dreams have to be broken.

My kids are experts in breaking things because they're careless. That's not the way God breaks a life. He's not careless with you; it's the opposite. He has so carefully planned your life that he knows the only way he can bless you is to break you. He's intentional.

A. W. Tozer says, "It is doubtful whether God can use a man greatly until He has hurt him deeply."[18] When we feel unqualified, we have to remember that God uses broken people to do big things. He's going to give you to the world, using you in the lives of others.

God is a giver by nature. "God so loved the world that he *gave* his one and only Son."[19] So if he's breaking you, it's because he desires to give you. He'll give you to your family. He'll give you to the poor and needy. He'll give you to your friends and neighbors who don't know him. He'll work through you by his power to accomplish his purpose.

In the Bible, God's hand represents his might. By the work of his hand, he created the world. By stretching out his hand, he saves the righteous and punishes the wicked. But as we see when Jesus committed his spirit into the Father's hands, those hands are also reaching out to tenderly receive and hold us.

Like the loaf of bread in Jesus's hands as he sat for supper in Emmaus, you are never out of God's hands. When he takes you out of your comfort zone, you are in his hands. When he blesses you, he's doing it with his hands. When he breaks you, the pieces of your life are still in his hands. Even when he gives you, distributing you to the world, you're not far from his hands. And he will eventually receive you back, just as he received his Son.

One time, Jesus was talking about his followers and the dangers they faced in life. He said, "My Father, who has given them to me, is greater than all; no one can snatch them out of my Father's hand."[20] We are safe in the Father's hands today. And we will be safe in the Father's hands for eternity. Knowing this, there is no detail of our lives too mundane or meaningless to submit to his care.

Practicing the Presence of God

In the 1620s a young French soldier named Nicholas Herman was walking outside one winter day when he came upon a tree that caught his attention. It was an ordinary tree. As ordinary as the bread Jesus broke at the table at Emmaus. As ordinary as your life and mine. But for some reason, Nicholas glimpsed some meaning that lay hidden within it.

Here was a tree that was barren of leaves or fruit, its spindly branches blowing stiffly in the wind. Yet when spring came, by God's plan it would begin to flourish. Leaves would bud out. Then flowers would develop and fruit would grow. New life was coming. It was a sure thing.

At once Nicholas saw an image of God's work in this. God brings life out of death.

A man who many years later interviewed Nicholas about this event reported, "This view had perfectly set him loose from the world, and kindled in him such a love for God, that he could not tell whether it had increased in above forty years that he had lived since."[21] In other words, this vision was a powerful start and sustaining revelation in Nicholas Herman's miraculous seven-mile journey. Like the disciples who received the bread from Jesus, his *eyes were opened*.

Eventually Nicholas would leave the army and join a Carmelite monastery in Paris, where he would choose for himself the new name Lawrence of the Resurrection. History, though, knows him better as Brother Lawrence.

Lawrence was of peasant origin and had little education, so he was given lowly jobs in the monastery working in the kitchen at first and later as a repairer of sandals. He didn't enjoy these kinds of work particularly, yet he did them with such joy and such peace, and his words were seasoned with such grace, that he gained a reputation for living near to God.

That's why Joseph de Beaufort, vicar general to the archbishop of Paris, came to the monastery to interview the then-elderly Lawrence. De Beaufort published the compilation of his interviews with Lawrence as *The Practice of the Presence of God*, a spiritual classic ever since.

We make coming to the love of God too complicated, said Lawrence to de Beaufort. We don't need complex theological theories. We don't need to get our religious practices just right. All we need is to do everything in our daily course of life out of love for God.

Summarizing Lawrence's view, de Beaufort said, "He had always been governed by love, without selfish views; and . . . having resolved to make the love of God the end of all his actions, he had found reasons to be well satisfied with his method. . . . He was pleased when he could take up a straw from the ground for the love of God, seeking Him only, and nothing else, not even His gifts."[22]

I don't know about you, but I want to learn how to turn the most ordinary actions of my life into a means of practicing being in the presence of God.

The apostle Paul had an extraordinary experience where he was "caught up to paradise and heard inexpressible things, things that no one is permitted to tell."[23] Others may have occasional experiences where they enjoy mystical union with God. But I believe that for most of us, most of the time, what we should be about is turning our everyday lives—going to school or work, taking care of the kids, taking the car in for an oil change—into a training ground for experiencing the practical presence of God.

Can you do the things you have in front of you today faithfully, not merely to fulfill a duty, not to gain notice from others, but because you love God and want to please him and live fully in your relationship with him? Making the beds can be as much a prayer as getting on your knees. Making dinner for your family can be as surely an act of worship as going to church to sing and lift your hands.

For Lawrence, practicing the presence of God was a discipline that was hard at first but got easier over time. You, too, can find that it becomes more natural to live every day in unity with God. Then when the time comes for you to cross the border from this life to the next life, it will be the same, only more. Much more so.

CONCLUSION

One More Step

The two followers' supper with Jesus in Emmaus came to an end before anyone had taken a bite. As soon as Cleopas and the other person recognized Jesus, he vanished. His point had been made. He had taught them about the Messiah from the Scriptures and had revealed himself to them as the risen Lord, and they would never think of him as a mere prophet ever again.

The two talked their situation over briefly and then hustled the seven miles back to Jerusalem. This return to Jerusalem was exactly what they were supposed to do. Jesus didn't want them to go back to their ordinary existence in a backwater village. He wanted them to renew their commitment to him and be there in the thick of what God was doing. I have little doubt that they were present in the upper room with Jesus's core group of 120 followers when the Holy Spirit descended at Pentecost, launching the church of Jesus.[1]

But what I want you to take note of is what they did when they first got back to Jerusalem. They found many of the surviving disciples and some other followers of Jesus gathered in a house. And they couldn't wait to spill the news to them. "The two told what had happened on the way, and how Jesus was recognized by them when he broke the bread."[2]

What happened immediately afterward is the most important thing of all: "While they were still talking about this, Jesus himself stood among them."[3]

So let's review . . .

The two people from Emmaus see Jesus.

They hurry to tell others about their experience.

The others see Jesus too.

Let me apply this to you and me in the simplest possible way. As we grow to see Jesus better and become more like him while we proceed in our own journey, let's tell others about him. As we're coming to see him clearer, they can as well.

Someone helped you get started on Mile 1 of your journey. Maybe now you can be that person for somebody else. Tell what has happened along the way as you have journeyed with Jesus. And help others see that Jesus invites them to walk with him too.

You have to make the journey for yourself. But you don't have to make it by yourself.

A Forty-Day Reading Guide to Jesus's Death and Resurrection

Use the following readings from the New Testament during the Lenten season (the days leading up to Easter) or at any time when you want to spend an extended period absorbing what Jesus went through for you. Think about the pattern it gives you to know God better.

Day 1. Jesus's last Passover—Matthew 26:1–5; Mark 14:1–2; Luke 22:1–2

Day 2. Judas's agreement to betray Jesus—Matthew 26:14–16; Mark 14:10–11; Luke 22:3–6

Day 3. A supper and service—Matthew 26:17–30; Mark 14:12–26; Luke 22:7–23; John 13:1–35

Day 4. The disciples' argument—Luke 22:24–30

Day 5. Prediction of Peter's denial—Matthew 26:31–35; Mark 14:27–31; Luke 22:31–39; John 13:36–38

Day 6. Jesus as the way to the Father—John 14:1–14

Day 7. The coming of the Holy Spirit—John 14:15–31

Day 8. Abiding in Jesus—John 15:1–17

Day 9. The hatred of the world—John 15:18–27

Day 10. The Spirit as a guide—John 16:1–15

Day 11. Grief into joy—John 16:16–33

Day 12. Jesus's prayer—John 17

Day 13. Anguished praying in Gethsemane—Matthew 26:36–46; Mark 14:32–42; Luke 22:40–46; John 18:1

Day 14. The betrayal—Matthew 26:47–56; Mark 14:43–52; Luke 22:47–53; John 18:2–11

Day 15. Jesus interrogated by Annas and Caiaphas as Peter disowns him—Matthew 26:57–58, 69–75; Mark 14:53–54, 66–72; Luke 22:54–65; John 18:12–27

Day 16. Jesus tried by the Sanhedrin—Matthew 26:59–68; Mark 14:55–65; Luke 22:66–71

Day 17. Jesus interrogated by Pontius Pilate—Matthew 27:1–2, 11–14; Mark 15:1–5; Luke 23:1–6; John 18:33–40

Day 18. Judas's death—Matthew 27:3–10

Day 19. Jesus interrogated by Herod Antipas—Luke 23:7–12

Day 20. Jesus accused and condemned—Matthew 27:15–26; Mark 15:6–15; Luke 23:13–25; John 18:29; 19:14–16

Day 21. Jesus mistreated by Roman soldiers—Matthew 27:27–31; Mark 15:16–20; Luke 23:36–37; John 19:1–3

Day 22. Jesus hanging on the cross—Matthew 27:32–38; Mark 15:21–28; Luke 23:26–34; John 19:17–24

Day 23. Bystanders mocking Jesus—Matthew 27:39–44; Mark 15:29–32; Luke 23:35–39

Day 24. A thief repents—Luke 23:40–43

Day 25. Mary, Jesus's mother, at the cross—John 19:25–27

Day 26. Darkness over the land—Matthew 27:45–53; Mark 15:33–38; Luke 23:44–45

Day 27. Jesus's death—Matthew 27:50; Mark 15:37; Luke 23:46; John 19:28–30

Day 28. Reaction by the bystanders—Matthew 27:54–56; Mark 15:39–41; Luke 23:47–49

Day 29. Jesus's side pierced—John 19:31–37

Day 30. Jesus buried—Matthew 27:57–61; Mark 15:42–47; Luke 23:50–56; John 19:38–42

Day 31. Guards placed at the tomb—Matthew 27:62–66

Day 32. Jesus risen—Matthew 28:1–10; Mark 16:1–11; Luke 24:1–12; John 20:1–18

Day 33. The guards' report—Matthew 28:11–15

Day 34. The two Jesus followers on the way to Emmaus—Mark 16:12–13; Luke 24:13–35

Day 35. Jesus's appearances to most of the disciples in Jerusalem—Mark 16:14–18; Luke 24:36–49; John 20:19–23

Day 36. Jesus's appearance to Thomas—John 20:24–29

Day 37. Jesus's appearance at the Sea of Galilee—John 21:1–23

Day 38. Jesus's appearance on a mountain in Galilee—Matthew 28:16–20

Day 39. The unrecorded works of Jesus—John 20:30–31; 21:24–25

Day 40. Jesus's ascension—Mark 16:19–20; Luke 24:50–53; Acts 1:3–11

Notes

Introduction: M.O.G.

1. See Luke 24:49.
2. See Mark 8:18.
3. See Luke 24:32.
4. Peter and Andrew: Matthew 4:19; Mark 1:17. Matthew (Levi): Matthew 9:9; Mark 2:14; Luke 5:27. Philip: John 1:43. The rich young ruler: Matthew 19:21; Mark 10:21; Luke 18:22. Other unnamed individuals: Matthew 8:19, 22; Luke 9:59.
5. John 13:36.
6. John 21:19, 22.
7. Matthew 28:19–20.
8. Matthew 16:24; Mark 8:34; Luke 9:23 (adding "daily"). See also Matthew 10:38, Luke 14:27, and John 12:26.
9. See John 10:4, 27.
10. See John 14:2.
11. John 14:5.
12. John 14:6.
13. Philippians 3:10–11.
14. Philippians 3:13–14.

A Word of Forgiveness

1. Luke 23:34.
2. Acts 3:15.

3. Matthew 5:44.

4. Hebrews 7:23–25.

5. See Romans 8:34; 1 John 2:1.

Mile 1: Get Your Slate Cleaned Here

1. William Cowper, "There Is a Fountain Filled with Blood," 1772.

2. 1 John 1:7. See also Hebrews 9:14 and Revelation 1:5.

3. Annie Lobert, "I Am Second," www.iamsecond.com/seconds /annie-lobert/. See also Annie Lobert, *Fallen: Out of the Sex Industry and into the Arms of the Savior* (Brentwood: Worthy, 2015).

4. Lobert, I Am Second.

5. Lobert, I Am Second.

6. Matthew 27:51.

7. Hebrews 10:19–22.

8. John 1:16, esv.

9. See Romans 6:1–2.

10. John Newton, Goodreads, www.goodreads.com/author /quotes/60149.John_Newton.

11. 1 John 1:8–9.

12. Matthew 6:14–15. See also Mark 11:25 and Luke 6:37.

13. Matthew 18:21.

14. Matthew 18:22.

15. Matthew 18:23–24, niv 1984.

16. Matthew 18:25.

17. Matthew 18:26.

18. Matthew 18:27.

19. Matthew 18:28, NIV 1984 and 2011

20. Matthew 18:29. Compare with Matthew 18:26.

21. Matthew 18:32–33.

22. Colossians 3:13.

23. Anne Lamott, *Traveling Mercies: Some Thoughts on Faith* (New York: Anchor Books, 1999), 134.

A Word of Salvation

1. See Mark 15:6–15.

2. Luke 23:32–33.

3. Isaiah 53:12.

4. See Psalm 22:6–8.

5. Luke 23:35.

6. Luke 23:37.

7. Luke 23:39.

8. See Matthew 27:44; Mark 15:32.

9. Luke 23:40–41.

10. Luke 23:42.

11. Luke 23:43.

12. See Romans 5:6–10; Colossians 1:21–23.

Mile 2: Ticket to Paradise

1. Genesis 40:7–8.

2. Genesis 40:14.

3. Genesis 40:23.

4. Genesis 41:9.

5. Luke 18:1–8.

6. Luke 18:1.

7. Luke 22:19.

8. Lamentations 3:21.

9. Lamentations 3:22–23.

A Word of Relationship

1. See Mark 14:27; Matthew 26:31, 56.

2. See Matthew 26:31–35, 69–75; Mark 14:27–31, 66–72; Luke 22:31–34, 54–62; John 18:15–18, 25–27.

3. See Matthew 27:1–10; Acts 1:18–19.

4. See John 20:19.

5. See Matthew 27:55–56; Mark 15:40–41; Luke 23:49.

6. John 19:25.

7. See Matthew 4:21; 27:56; Mark 15:40.

8. See Luke 2:19, 51.

9. John 13:23; 19:26; 20:2; 21:7, 20, 24.

10. John 19:26–27.

11. See Matthew 13:55–56.

12. See Mark 3:21.

13. Acts 1:14; 1 Corinthians 15:7. One brother, James, would eventually become the leader of the Christian church (Acts 12:17; 15:13; 21:18; Galatians 1:19; 2:9, 12). James and another brother, Jude, would write the New Testament books that bear their names (James 1:1; Jude 1:1). In humility, James and Jude both chose to refer to themselves in their letters as servants of Jesus, rather than claiming their

status as his brothers. It reminds me of John referring to himself indirectly as the disciple whom Jesus loved.

14. Matthew 12:48–50. See also Matthew 10:34–37; Mark 3:31–35; Luke 8:19–21. If John was Jesus's cousin, as it appears, then that makes Jesus's decision less unusual, because he was keeping his mother under the care of extended family. He was entrusting Mary to her nephew.

Mile 3: The Jesus of Nazareth Adoption Agency

1. Miller McPherson, Lynn Smith-Lovin, and Matthew E. Brashears, "Social Isolation in America: Changes in Core Discussion Networks over Two Decades." *American Sociological Review* 71, no. 3 (June 2006): 353–75.

2. Julianne Holt-Lunstad et al, "Loneliness and Social Isolation as Risk Factors for Mortality: A Meta-Analytic Review." *Perspectives on Psychological Science* 10, no. 2 (March 2015): 227–37.

3. Ethan Kross et al, "Facebook Use Predicts Declines in Subjective Well-Being in Young Adults," *PLoS ONE* 8, no. 8 (August 14, 2013): http://journals.plos.org/plosone/article?id=10.1371/journal.pone.0069841.

4. See Genesis 2:18, 21–22.

5. Mark 8:33.

6. Matthew 15:16.

7. Matthew 17:17.

8. Matthew 6:30; 8:26; 14:31; 16:8; 17:20; Luke 12:28.

9. Luke 24:25.

10. See John 16:8–11.

11. Romans 8:1–2.

12. Romans 8:14–16. See also Galatians 4:4–7.

13. Ephesians 1:4–5.

14. Galatians 3:26.

15. See Matthew 14:23; Mark 1:35.

16. See Luke 6:12.

17. See Matthew 26:36–46; Mark 14:32–42; Luke 22:39–46.

18. Ephesians 2:19.

19. John 17:20–21, 23.

20. Hebrews 2:11.

21. The New Testament describes us as one another's spiritual parents and children as well as one another's spiritual brothers and sisters (see 1 Timothy 5:1–2).

22. See Matthew 7:9–10.

23. Galatians 3:28.

A Word of Abandonment

1. See Luke 22:53.

2. Matthew 27:45. For the whole episode, see Matthew 27:45–50 or Mark 15:33–37.

3. Matthew 27:46.

4. Deuteronomy 21:23.

5. Galatians 3:13.

6. See John 1:29, 36.

7. See Matthew 20:28; Mark 10:45.

8. 1 Corinthians 5:7. See also 1 Peter 1:18–19.

9. See Isaiah 53:4–6, 10–12.

10. 2 Corinthians 5:21.

Mile 4: Godforsaken

1. Mother Teresa, *Come Be My Light: The Private Writings of the Saint of Calcutta,* ed. Brian Kolodiejchuk (New York: Doubleday, 2006), 210.

2. See Matthew 26:36–46; Mark 14:32–42; Luke 22:39–46; John 18:1.

3. Matthew 26:39.

4. Matthew 26:39.

5. See Luke 22:39.

6. See Psalm 23:1–4.

7. Hebrews 13:5. See also Deuteronomy 31:6, 8 and Joshua 1:5.

8. Chris Tomlin, "You Are My King," *Authentic* (1998).

9. Matthew 1:23.

10. Revelation 1:8.

11. John 14:18.

12. 2 Corinthians 4:17.

13. Genesis 39:20–21.

14. Proverbs 18:24.

A Word of Distress

1. John 19:28.

2. Psalm 22:15.

3. Hebrews 2:14.

4. See Matthew 27:45–50; Mark 15:33–37.

5. John 19:28.

6. See Matthew 27:33–34; Mark 15:22–23.

7. John 19:29.

8. See Exodus 12:21–23.

9. See Leviticus 14:1–7, 33–53.

10. Psalm 51:7.

Mile 5: Parched

1. John 16:33.

2. See Exodus 17:1–7.

3. Numbers 20:2–13.

4. 1 Corinthians 10:4.

5. 2 Corinthians 12:7.

6. 2 Corinthians 11:23–28.

7. Colossians 1:24.

8. 2 Corinthians 4:7.

9. 2 Corinthians 4:10–11.

10. 2 Corinthians 12:9.

11. 2 Corinthians 12:10.

12. Anna Bartlett Warner, "Jesus Loves Me," 1860.

13. See John 4:4–26.

14. John 4:10.

15. John 4:11.

16. See John 6:1–13.

17. John 4:13–14.

18. John 4:15.

19. John 4:16.

20. John 4:17.

21. John 4:25.

22. John 4:26.

23. See Jeremiah 2:13.

24. Adapted from Samuel Taylor Coleridge, "The Rime of the Ancient Mariner," part 2, 1834.

25. Psalm 63:1. See also Psalm 42:1–2.

26. Isaiah 55:1.

27. Revelation 7:16–17.

A Word of Triumph

1. John 19:30.

2. John 17:4.

3. John 19:28, emphasis added.

4. See John 19:30.

5. See Genesis 3:15.

Mile 6: Out of the Jaws of Defeat

1. John 20:13.

2. 2 Corinthians 4:8–9.

3. Elvina M. Hall, "Jesus Paid It All," 1865.

4. See Ephesians 2:1–9.

5. See Psalm 46:10, NASB.

6. See John 19:2–3.

7. See John 19:19–22.

8. See 1 Corinthians 9:24–27.

9. See 1 Peter 5:1–4.

10. See James 1:12; Revelation 2:8–10.

11. 2 Timothy 4:6–8.

12. 2 Timothy 2:11–12.

13. Ephesians 3:20.

14. Romans 8:28.

15. Colossians 1:20.

16. John 16:33.

17. 1 John 5:4–5.

18. Romans 8:31–35, 37–39.

19. 1 Corinthians 15:26.

20. Hebrews 2:14–15.

21. 1 Corinthians 15:54.

22. 1 Corinthians 15:55.

23. 1 Corinthians 15:57.

24. 1 Corinthians 15:58.

25. Revelation 21:6.

26. Revelation 21:6–7.

A Word of Reunion

1. John 13:3. See also John 16:5, 10, 28; 17:11, 13.

2. See John 14:2–3.

3. Luke 23:46.

4. John 10:17–18.

5. See Philippians 2:5–11.

Mile 7: Into the Presence of God

1. Revelation 21:3.

2. John 17:3. See also John 3:16, 36; 4:14; 5:24; 6:40, 47; 1 John 5:11–12.

3. Galatians 6:8.

4. 1 Timothy 6:12.

5. 1 Corinthians 13:12.

6. 2 Corinthians 5:7.

7. John 20:29.

8. Luke 24:28–32.

9. Luke 24:30–31.

10. Luke 24:31.

11. Luke 22:15–16.

12. Revelation 19:9, NASB.

13. Ephesians 5:25–27.

14. Luke 24:30.

15. See Luke 9:16.

16. See Luke 22:19. Paul found these actions significant enough to remind people of them in 1 Corinthians 11:23–24.

17. See Exodus 2:10.

18. A. W. Tozer, *The Root of the Righteous: Tapping the Bedrock of True Spirituality* (1955; reprint, Camp Hill, PA: WingSpread Publishers, 2006), 165.

19. John 3:16, emphasis added.

20. John 10:29.

21. Brother Lawrence, first conversation, *The Practice of the Presence of God: The Best Rule of Holy Life* (London: Epworth, 1933), Christian Classics Ethereal Library, www.ccel.org/ccel/lawrence/practice.iii.i.html.

22. Brother Lawrence, second conversation, www.ccel.org/ccel/lawrence/practice.iii.ii.html.

23. 2 Corinthians 12:4.

Conclusion: One More Step

1. Acts 1:15; 2–4.

2. Luke 24:35.

3. Luke 24:36.

DVD AND PARTICIPANT'S GUIDE

ALSO AVAILABLE!

Experience the power and meaning of the last words of Christ with your family, your small group, or in your personal devotions.

MULTNOMAH